15 REASONS people voted for Trump in 2016

and why these don't apply in 2020

by

Steve Dow

ISBN 978-1-7332510-2-0
Broad Vine Press
broadvinepress.com

Dedication:

To those of us who still care enough to try…

Contents

Introduction

This book is predominately written in the first two weeks of June 2019, during nights after work and on weekends. As is the case with the news cycle these days, one can't help but sense that some huge bombshell headline is always just around the corner, waiting to pounce. I very much have this feeling while writing this, but I don't know what that bombshell might be, and I have real doubts that some among us would even know or care anymore when it comes. This foreboding sense about the future is a big reason for my writing this, as I at least want to capture my thoughts right now.

If you are reading this before the 2020 U.S. election, perhaps things have changed for the better in ways that I could not foresee when I wrote this... making some of the arguments in this writing less relevant. That would be a very welcomed surprise.

Sadly, however, I expect the opposite will occur and that the many reasons for concern discussed herein will be supported with additional examples, further justifying that concern. After experiencing two and a half years of the current president in office, the patterns exhibited show no sign of changing.

And in the event that this president somehow finds a way to extend his stay even beyond a second term in 2024 (which he hints at frequently), I suspect that the concerns listed herein will be exponentially magnified at that time.

<u>Disclosure</u>:

I am not a Democrat and never have been. I wish I lived in a world where I did not feel the need to disclose that... a world where my intended audience would simply take my words on their own merit. In truth, though, we all know this is not the world we live in. People care so much about which political team you are on that many would immediately dismiss me if they suspected I was a Democrat. My political team is "no team," as I have been "No Party Preference" since I could vote. I don't need anyone to tell me what my platform should be. I can do that on my own.

<u>Note about intended audience:</u>

This book is addressed to those people who are considering voting for Trump in 2020 but are not sure if they will do so. It is <u>not</u> geared to those who have jumped on the Trump train with no concern for where the train is going or whether the wheels are falling off. I doubt I'd be able to really influence such unquestioning Trump supporters anyway... but hope springs eternal.

I am also purposefully staying away from the racist, anti-immigrant, misogynistic, and Islamophobic claims against Trump in this book. Although there are volumes of writing (and actual video tape) to support that many of these claims are valid, I suspect that my intended audience is jaded by such claims and may consider some of them overzealous accusations by those on the left (which some may indeed be). Besides, there is plenty to discuss about Trump beyond these accusations that should give voters pause.

Note to intended audience:

There are many reasons why I did not vote for Trump in 2016, but I understand why he was elected and why some voters (perhaps you) found him appealing. I ask that you read through the 15 reasons noted in this book, that you truly try to absorb the points being made, and that you be open to letting them impact your thinking. If you did vote for Trump in 2016 for one of the noted reasons, what is your take on that reasoning now? Did your vote produce the result you wanted in relation to that reason? Is the reason still valid for 2020? It is my hope that this short book can convince you that the reasons given for voting for Trump in 2016 are not good reasons now.

I think it is important for me as writer to be able to walk the reader through how I came to believe what I believe. In multiple places throughout this writing, I reference specific articles that either provided me with data or helped me further formulate my understanding. I did not reference every such data source in the text, but a listing of sources is included at the end of the book.

Proclaimed Reasons for a 2016 Trump Vote

01. "Trump is unconventional."

This was clearly a drawing point for some voters. People were tired of "establishment" politicians and they wanted to shake things up with a shock to the system.

<u>2019 Update</u>:
Well, the 2016 presidential election absolutely was a shock to the system and the "shake-things-up" vote has definitely been registered. This goal of jolting career politicians to think differently may have been met, but I suspect not in the way many of these voters wanted. If the idea was to get "politicians to stop being politicians," this vote was a failure. What it has done is simply get some politicians to strategize their marketing spin differently -- to stress the unconventional or outsider aspects of their backgrounds. The "establishment" simply changed shirts. To use a popular metaphor: if you see politicians as 'pigs', this shock simply caused some to put on lipstick. In some rare occasions, weasels may have replaced pigs, but is that really an improvement?

This last paragraph may seem harsh. In truth, I do not see most politicians in the bad light listed above (weasels and pigs). Politicians are human beings with human faults. I believe more politicians care about public service than people are willing to admit, but it is also true that the self-serving nature of many of them are so frequently on display. Trump has done nothing to improve that. I do not see that he has ushered in any more people with the public-service mindset. In fact, it seems to me the exact opposite has happened. The swamp is not drained, but further flooded and new alligators now swim in the waters.

My Ask:

The 2016 election shook things, but how much more shaking do you want? It is one thing to attempt shock therapy to hopefully induce a reevaluation of how we govern ourselves. It is quite another to find ways to extend a very damaging earthquake.

Trump has certainly been unconventional. He is a bull in a china shop... and you know it. He does not plan like we'd want our elected leaders to plan, he is distracted by the smallest of things, and he behaves like an eight-year-old spoiled kid... and, again, you know it. I ask that you recognize this fact.

02. "Trump tells-it-like-it-is."

This was another big one for people. Trump is not "politically correct" and many found that refreshing. There were times when I even admired that about him, although other times, I found it horrifying… it really depended on the circumstance.

2019 Update:
"Trump tells it like it is???" Oh, really now!?

We know that this is completely false. Don't confuse Trump's bluntness and rudeness with "telling it like it is." "Telling it like it is" inherently requires that the person tell the truth.

Trump has been shown to lie or mislead at an absolutely absurd rate. The *Washington Post* "Trump-Lie-Tracker" [1] website has documented 10,111 such instances since Trump was inaugurated president through April 27, 2019. That equates to approximately 375 such instances each month, more than 12 per day. Assuming he gets six hours of sleep per night, that equates to 1 falsehood every 90 minutes of his waking day… and keep in mind these are only the documented instances. Who knows how many lies he tells behind closed doors?

OK, so you don't like the *Washington Post*? Let's look at another source. *PolitiFact.com* graded both Trump[2] and

---

[1] https://www.washingtonpost.com/graphics/politics/trump-claims-database/?utm_term=.ddde6422f5cc

[2] https://www.politifact.com/personalities/donald-trump/

Obama[3] regarding truthfulness. Obama got an untruthfulness score (telling "mostly false, false, or 'pants-on-fire'-false" statements) of 24%. Trump's grade for untruthfulness, by comparison, was 70% -- nearly 3 times worse than Obama's.

OK, so you don't like the *Washington Post* or *PolitiFact*? Then please just look with your own eyes and listen with your own ears. If you don't recognize this about him, you are likely a Trump cultist and simply do not want to admit it. Please snap out of it.

My Ask:

Please stop with the "all politicians lie" false equivalency. Recognize what lying at this rate does to the trust in the institution of the presidency, and the country's standing in the world by extension.

[3] https://www.politifact.com/personalities/barack-obama/

03. "Hillary Clinton is mentally ill."

This one surprised me to hear back in 2016, but Trump did indeed claim[4] that Hillary Clinton's brain had "short-circuited" and he questioned her brain function in general.

2019 Update:
I found this one immediately laughable back in 2016, yet some people appeared to take this as a legitimate concern. I was not a huge fan of Hillary Clinton, yet she was clearly a very smart person, with obvious control of her brain's executive function. She may have had miscellaneous health issues like we all do, but she was not mentally ill.

Having this claim come from Trump was specifically rich. As stated previously, there is documentable evidence that Trump lies at an absolutely stunning rate. Try to imagine yourself in the mind of someone who tells a documented lie or falsehood every hour and a half. Does this person know that he is lying, and he just doesn't care... or perhaps the lines between reality and fantasy are truly a bit blurred for him? You might think this goes too far to say, but please think on this one for a while.

When a person is documented telling SO MANY untruths each and every day, it becomes more and more reasonable to believe that perhaps this person believes the untruths he is spewing. It is absolutely reasonable to have concerns that he is not functioning with a full deck. The idea that we might make this person the most powerful person in the world (for

[4] http://nymag.com/intelligencer/2016/08/trump-questions-clintons-mental-health.html

another term) should at the least cause pause for every voter.

Trump has proclaimed himself an "extremely stable genius," yet his behavior is demonstrably erratic, and he has taken legal action to prevent his alma mater schools from releasing his educational transcripts. Why hide your grades if you are such a genius? Most notable about this statement, though is that no one who is an extremely stable genius would ever say something remotely like, "I am an extremely stable genius," or another favorite, that China likes him for his "very, very large brain."

Come on. You MUST see this. This is crazy!

Also note the relevant discussion regarding Trump and Narcissistic Personality Disorder (NPD). Psychologists typically avoid making a formal diagnosis without first meeting with the subject, but note that Donald Trump without question checks every relevant box on the NPD checklist[5]... and the check marks are made with the darkest of permanent marker... no light pencil-marks needed.

I've heard some imply that all politicians are narcissists and I understand their general argument. I don't doubt that there are multiple U.S. politicians meeting the NPD criteria, but it is a clear exaggeration to say that this is every politician. It is also an exaggeration to suggest that others frequently rise to the level of narcissism exhibited by Trump on a daily basis.

---

[5] https://www.psychologytoday.com/us/blog/the-human-beast/201608/does-trump-suffer-narcissistic-personality-disorder

My Ask:

Please recognize that Trump is starting up the same tactics again for 2020. He is deflecting very justified concerns about his own mental stability by infantile name-calling of his political opponents. Now that there is no Hillary Clinton to run against, Trump is turning his "they're crazy" strategy on his new opponents. At one time, he spoke highly of Bernie Sanders. Now, Bernie is "Crazy Bernie." Also, Joe Biden is now "Crazy Joe Biden" (although Trump now seems to prefer "Sleepy Joe").

This is par for the course with Trump. Other nicknames include: "Crazy Nancy (Pelosi)," "Wacky Jacky (Rosen)," "Crazy Maxine (Waters)," and "Wacky Congresswoman Wilson (Frederica Wilson)." If you want more evidence of Trump's childish and non-presidential behavior, just check the entire page dedicated solely to Trump's name-calling on Wikipedia[6].

I ask that you recognize what Trump is doing when he plays this stupid game. He is deflecting from himself and he is trying to get you to think "Crazy Nancy" when you see Nancy Pelosi. This is "Branding 101." He was effective with branding Hillary Clinton as "Crooked Hillary" for example. Whether you wanted to think it or not, when you heard "Crooked" you thought "Hillary" ... even if only on a subconscious level.

Like or dislike an opponent's policy positions as you will, but please don't fall for this game. Trump would have you believe that all of his opponents are crazy, yet he – despite

[6] https://en.wikipedia.org/wiki/List_of_nicknames_used_by_Donald_Trump

his erratic behavior and frequent self-contradictions[7] – is somehow the epitome of stable "geniushood." If you do feel that you were fooled by this claim in 2016, I ask that you don't allow yourself to be fooled again. Please don't take the bait in 2020.

[7] https://www.politico.com/magazine/story/2016/05/donald-trump-2016-contradictions-213869

04. "Trump is an excellent businessman."

Having grown up in New Jersey, I watched New York City local news and I recall learning about Trump's many failures as a businessman decades ago: (a) his Atlantic City casino going bankrupt, (b) his Trump airline going out of business, and (c) his gamble in the courts that effectively ended the United States Football League (USFL), are some that come to mind. He liked to brag and to flaunt himself, but it was apparent to anyone I knew interested in discussing the matter that he was an obvious conman.

I did begin to like Trump on NBC's "Apprentice" television show (starting in 2004) as I certainly found him to be entertaining on it. This is indeed a credit to the charm that Trump can effectively display. He could be charismatic and funny, but I was always able to separate Trump the entertainer and self-promoter from Trump the very suspect businessman.

2019 Update:

- Business and Government -

I fully appreciate and share the desire to have governments learn best practices from the business world. Personally, I have learned some tricks of the trade as an MBA graduate and owner of my own company, and I have – in a very small way – had some success locally transferring business knowledge to government agencies. Where governments can become more efficient, we need to push for that, and we should implement required "continuous-improvement" procedures for each governmental department.

This said, it should be clear that I am not at all against supporting a businessperson as the country's leader. That person, however, must understand that the country IS NOT a company. The rules are different, and the very mission is different.

Many business leaders today only think in the short-term anyway. They want to raise a stock price so they can cash out and hit the beach for the rest of their lives. Good business leaders think long-term for the company. A president (business background or not) must have a similar long-term vision, and Trump clearly lacks this. He has consistently shown that he is distracted minute-by-minute and that he is not able to stay focused on anything that does not impact him personally.

- Trump's Business Losses –

The New York Times (NY Times) has unleashed devasting reporting within the last few years regarding Donald Trumps' business acumen (or lack thereof) and the staggering amount of money he has lost over the years. It is true that Trump still refuses to release his tax returns – making details about his finances more difficult to know for sure. You can't help but wonder why he is so adamant about hiding this from the public – especially since he previously indicated he would have no problem releasing them.[8] People seem to have forgotten that part.

---

[8] https://money.cnn.com/2017/04/17/news/donald-trump-tax-returns/index.html

According to the October 2, 2018, New York Times article[9], Trump took in approximately *"$413 million in today's dollars from his father's real estate empire."* Trump had discussed taking a *"small loan"* from his father of $1 million… so it looks like he was off by just…let me see… this minus that… carry the one… A WHOLE LOT! An analysis posted in Wikipedia[10] reads as follows:

"A 2016 analysis of Trump's business career in The Economist concluded that his performance since 1985 had been 'mediocre compared with the stock market and property in New York.' A subsequent analysis in The Washington Post similarly noted that Trump's estimated net worth of $100 million in 1978 would have increased to $6 billion by 2016 if he had invested it in a typical retirement fund…'."

Forbes recently listed Trump's worth at $3.1 billion, but this information should be tempered against the April 20, 2018 Washington Post (WP) article[11], which showed how Trump supposedly would purposefully exaggerate his wealth for such publications. If you do trust this Forbes number and you think the WP $6 billion number is "fake news," feel free to cut it in half. Doing so still implies that Trump did not need to do much at all to get to his claimed worth of $3.1 billion given the money he was gifted from his father's businesses. Despite what he'd have you believe, Trump never was able to free his mouth from the silver spoon.

---

[9] https://www.nytimes.com/interactive/2018/10/02/us/politics/donald-trump-tax-schemes-fred-trump.html?module=inline

[10] https://en.wikipedia.org/wiki/Wealth_of_Donald_Trump#Investment_performance

[11] https://www.washingtonpost.com/outlook/trump-lied-to-me-about-his-wealth-to-get-onto-the-forbes-400-here-are-the-tapes/2018/04/20/ac762b08-4287-11e8-8569-26fda6b404c7_story.html

The New York Times continues with a blistering May 8, 2019 report[12], detailing some of Trump's business losses. Regarding the period from 1985-1994, the NY Times writes the following:

> *"The numbers show that in 1985, Mr. Trump reported losses of $46.1 million from his core businesses — largely casinos, hotels and retail space in apartment buildings. They continued to lose money every year, totaling $1.17 billion in losses for the decade. In fact, year after year, Mr. Trump appears to have lost more money than nearly any other individual American taxpayer, The Times found when it compared his results with detailed information the I.R.S. compiles on an annual sampling of high-income earners.*
>
> *His core business losses in 1990 and 1991 — more than $250 million each year — were more than double those of the nearest taxpayers in the I.R.S. information for those years."*

Trump called the NY Times report a "highly inaccurate Fake News hit job!" but he never pointed out which parts of the deeply researched story were "fake." He even corroborated the purported "fake news" saying via Twitter that these were "losses for tax purposes," implying that they were purposeful. Trump, the self-described "king of debt," would indicate how an annual loss can be useful for businesses – inferring of course that all us lowly folk are simply too stupid to understand the concept of a tax write-off.

---

[12] https://www.nytimes.com/interactive/2019/05/07/us/politics/donald-trump-taxes.html

There is a difference, however, between timing smart business investments to optimize tax write-offs and taking tax write-offs because you continually lose money due to mismanagement. The first scenario is smart. The second is not. Bragging about this second scenario as Trump has done is akin to bragging that you turned down a doubling of your salary because you didn't want to pay taxes on the excess income. It is stupid.

Factor this all in with Trump having run six separate companies into bankruptcy[13], and the argument that Trump is an "excellent businessman" becomes quite a difficult argument to defend.

My Ask:

Please realize that Trump is an excellent marketer and self-promoter. He is not an excellent businessman. The "to-hell-with-you," risky negotiating tactics that he is known for may have seemed OK to him when dealing with an architect that he did not want to pay, but using those types of tactics in national and global politics has already destabilized much of the political discourse internally and with our allies. The consequences could be quite dangerous.

---

[13] https://www.thoughtco.com/donald-trump-business-bankruptcies-4152019

05. "Trump will work hard."

During the campaign leading up to the 2016 election, Trump frequently attacked President Obama for taking vacations and golfing. Trump, he said, would be too busy working for the American people to take vacations.

2019 Update:

Well… that's a laugh. It is hard to believe someone would have the gall to make such a statement in a campaign and then so obviously do the exact opposite of what he said he'd do, but that is Trump for you. This is such a blatant lie that someone has actually made an entire website – trumpgolfcount.com[14] – dedicated to tracking it.

This website shows that after 123 weeks in office, President Obama was confirmed playing golf 72 times. President Trump, meanwhile, was confirmed playing golf 84 times – but in truth "likely played" a total of 135 times – during this same 123-week period.

Understand that this "likely played golf" component to the analysis is a direct offshoot to Trump's lack of transparency here. I suppose it is understandable that he would want to downplay the number of his golf outings in light of his earlier attacks on Obama. The costs for his golf outings[15] also appear to be significantly more than costs related to Obama's golf time.

---

[14] https://trumpgolfcount.com/

[15] https://www.newsweek.com/trump-golf-102-million-report-1432550

Ultimately, do I care that the president likes to play golf? No, not really. Do I care that he blatantly lied about golf? Yes, I do... but with this just being one lie on top of thousands, that in itself is no shock here for me. This lie though does highlight something else that I think is important... namely, his very poor work ethic.

It seems very clear to me that Donald Trump is, at best, disinterested in doing the hard work of being president. He escapes to the golf course or his Mar a Lago estate whenever he can. He takes significant "executive time" in his workday. There is even evidence in the Mueller Report that Trump did not expect to – and perhaps did not even want to – win the presidency. He may have simply viewed his campaign as a means to strengthen his brand worldwide, never expecting to inherent the work required of a president.

My Ask:

Trump likes the pomp and circumstance of the presidency... but not the work. Look no further than the May 22, 2019 meeting about infrastructure when Trump walked out before even sitting down. He says he could not meet with Congressional leaders to discuss the very important issue of crumbling infrastructure in the country because these political rivals were rightfully alarmed by the Mueller Report and they – given their sworn duty to provide oversight – were therefore following up on leads in that report.

I ask that you see this for what it is. This is a president who is refusing to uphold the oath he took when sworn into office. That alone should bring the “I”-word (his nickname for “impeachment”) into consideration. But even if you don’t think impeachment should be considered, do at least acknowledge that this man is finding excuses not to work.

06. "Trump will defend us & be tough on our adversaries."

I get it. Historically, Republicans are viewed as the tough-guys and Democrats are the hippy beatniks. I've always found that as unfair, outdated, and frequently incorrect, but we as a nation have never fully snapped out of the 1960's 'hawk vs dove' mindset, and R vs D politics is an obvious case where this claimed duality plays out. If you want someone to be tough with our adversaries, the default position for many is to vote Republican.

Trump talked like a tough guy during the 2016 campaign and I'd venture to guess that some of you may have even been turned off a bit by it, but you ultimately held out hope that he would be a 'tough guy' for the country. To quote a former client regarding one of his "problem employees," you may have thought: *"He may be an asshole... but he's <u>my</u> asshole."* (I always found that quote crudely funny, if not also a bit distracting and too thought-provoking in a bad way). Regardless, the inferred point of the quote is that one's "assholeness" could be a useful weapon for good.

<u>2019 Update</u>:

After two years in office, it turns out this does not apply to Trump. He is not a tough guy at all. He is a tough talker, but he is spineless when the rubber meets the road.

What else do you call an American president who glosses over the premeditated murder of U.S. resident and *Washington Post* journalist Jamal Khashoggi, which was carried out in 2018 under the order of the Saudi Prince Mohammed bin Salman?

Trumps' official statement included the following:

"Our intelligence agencies continue to assess all information, but it could very well be that the Crown Prince had knowledge of this tragic event – maybe he did and maybe he didn't! That being said, we may never know all of the facts surrounding the murder of Mr. Jamal Khashoggi."

The public evidence, however, overwhelmingly points to the prince as directing this murder, and the CIA came to this same conclusion quickly, yet Trump wanted to "further investigate" ... indefinitely, it appears. Jared Kushner in an Axios interview aired on June 2, 2019, indicated that the investigation is still ongoing – a full 8 months after Khashoggi's murder! This is clear stalling. I can't think of a more cowardly thing to do in this situation that this. (As an aside, I also can't help but wonder what Trump's reaction would have been if Khashoggi worked for Fox News).

Now if you don't think Trump is a coward for doing this, you must concede that this in no way depicts him as being "tough on our adversaries." If you are saying to yourself that Saudi Arabia is not an adversary, please review the facts here. Members of the Saudi government purposefully murdered an unarmed U.S. resident because he spoke truth to power as a journalist. Although one or more of those who physically carried out the murder may face some level of justice as fall-guys, the person that directed the crime most certainly will not. Saudi Arabia also: (a) was the home to the vast majority of 9/11 hijackers, (b) requires that women must have permission from a male "guardian" to travel, work, or go to school, and (c) allows for homosexuals to be killed if they are sexually active. If there is any country that is worthy of a relationship-reevaluation, it is Saudi Arabia.

Trump is placating Saudi Arabia, and the potential reasons for doing so are eyebrow-raising. Trump and/or his family have had (and still have, via the Trump hotel in DC) significant and surprising business dealing with Saudi Arabia, yet he continues to claim that there is "nothing to see here." Most disturbingly, he continues to arm the Saudis – even potentially with nuclear technology. Even Republicans[16], including Senators "Lindsey Graham, Todd Young, and Rand Paul were not comfortable with that.

I will also remind you that Trump placates other adversaries as well. Despite the on-again-off-again bromance with Kim Jong-un of North Korea, Trump frequently kisses up to him. It is now clear that Kim continues his nuclear/missile program, yet Trump suddenly acts like it is no big deal after all... despite all his "rocket man," tough-guy antics on Twitter.

Trumps' performance in Helsinki in July 2018 during his meeting with Vladimir Putin is perhaps the biggest example of Trump's lack of backbone. Despite unanimous consent between the U.S. Director of National Intelligence, the National Security Agency (NSA), the Federal Bureau of

---

[16] https://www.businessinsider.com/trump-saudi-arabia-iran-weapons-republicans-national-security-risks-2019-6

Investigation (FBI), and the Central Intelligence Agency (CIA) that Russia was responsible for a campaign to influence the election (using illegal means to do so), Trump threw up his hands, and publicly voiced his trust of Putin over his own intelligence agencies.

Why would a President of the United States possibly do this!? Well… because Putin said he didn't do it. But… why would the President of the United States trust a former KGB-spy over the word of all U.S. intelligence agencies!? Because when Putin said it, he said it… *"very firmly."*

Oh, well… I see… if he said it *firmly*… especially *very firmly*, then that is different. Why didn't Trump just say so from the very beginning!?

Jokes aside, the only adequate response to Trump during that news conference is *"what a weenie!"* This was an absolute embarrassment to the U.S. Even ardent Trump loyalists took to social media to admit that this was not Trump's best day. You think!?

My Ask:

Please recognize that Trump is not a tough guy. He is a child who plays dress-up, pretending to be a tough guy. He shows no backbone with people that should be called on the carpet, he praises people for committing and/or encouraging human rights violations (such as Duterte in the Philippines), and he is rarely capably of acting like an adult with our actual allies.

I also ask that you read the Mueller Report... or at least that you download the free audiobook and listen to it in the car. Mueller was not able to get access to all the information he would have liked to have had regarding the possibility of Trump collusion with Russia. Perhaps because of this, he did not find enough evidence to charge Trump with conspiracy (which is a very high legal bar to clear). Concerning evidence, however, does indeed exist. Whether conspiracy with Russia will eventually be proven or not, it is quite clear that the actions that Trump has taken (such as destabilizing NATO) has frequently been in line with actions one might take if they were inclined to do Putin's bidding. That should be concerning for all voters in 2020.

07. "Trump will support the military."

Disclosure:

I did not serve in the military. I did not have siblings or parents that enlisted in the military. I grew up in a family where college was the expectation and military service was not typically discussed as an option. I was too young to serve in the First Gulf War and I was getting married and/or in night school for my MBA when the post-9/11 wars in Afghanistan and Iraq started. Perhaps things may have been different if the timing was different, but in all honesty, I don't know that they would have been.

The truth is I have long had three reservations regarding military service. First, I didn't know if I had the necessary courage; second, I grew up learning about the Vietnam War and I developed a high level of skepticism regarding leaders' motivations for entering wars in the first place; and third, I did not want to be in a situation where I might kill innocent people.

In truth, I'm not sure which if the three reservations was strongest, but they played off each other. I would not want to ship off to war thinking I was "fighting for freedom" when in truth I was fighting for some lesser purpose (such as oil rights). I felt I'd be wasting my life to die for something like oil. On the flip side, though, I know that my questioning of war motives (and my focus on the potential for killing innocents) also provided me an escape hatch, whereby I could justify my staying away – wondering internally if this doubled as a convenient excuse to be a coward.

Having made this confession, I suspect that some may feel I am disqualified from even expressing an opinion on the military. I do not share that view. I recognize that war may be a necessary evil in some circumstances, but I care about doing the best we can to avoid war – for the sake of people on both sides of a potential conflict. I am in awe of the courage shown by people who enlist knowing they may be putting their lives on the line, and I see it as essential that such courageous lives not be lost on anything unworthy of such a sacrifice.

2019 Update:

OK, back to Trump. This one goes hand in hand with "Trump will defend us & be tough on our adversaries." Trump talks a big game when he wants to. He clearly likes being associated with the bravery of soldiers. He wants a military parade and he loves saluting soldiers – even a North Korean general at one point. From a practical standpoint, he clearly wants the "guys with guns" on his side, so he aims to say what he thinks are the right things to say to the military.

He can indeed even say the right things at times (or at least he can read what has been prepared for him), as he did today on June 6, 2019 during a speech commemorating the 75th anniversary of D-Day in France. It would have perhaps been best though if he chose to stay silent before and after the speech, as he was back to his petty self, complaining about things like what the celebrity-of-the-day wrote about him on Twitter.

We have learned some things about Trump, and they are worth repeating.

(1) Trump did not serve in Vietnam due to a claimed medical ineligibility (bone spurs), but there is significant evidence that his father convinced a doctor to fill out that ineligibility paperwork. In his own words, Trump was "always the best athlete" so being medically ineligible would be quite the surprise (that is, if he was not the son of a multi-millionaire). Again, I did not serve in the military so if my calling out Trump on this does not sit well with you, I understand that. That does not, however, change anything written above.

(2) Trump was haunted by John McCain in life, and apparently still is several months after McCain's death. Senator McCain was a tortured prisoner of war who had an opportunity to leave captivity but chose to stay and keep getting tortured because he did not want to leave his fellow soldiers behind. Trump famously mocked McCain on numerous occasions during and after McCain's life, but he did not limit his mocking to war heroes. Recall that he mocked the families of war heroes as well by mocking the parents of Humayun Khan, a U.S. soldier killed in battle. Trump took extensive criticism for how he dealt with these Gold Star parents and never seemed to learn from that criticism.

In truth though, we knew all this about Trump before the 2016 election, yet people still voted for him. So, what has he done for the military while in office? Maybe he has changed his tune a bit? Maybe his actions show that he really cares for the military? ... don't hold your breath.

- What is Trump doing for military families now? –

Is he really helping military families? Well, let's look. He certainly says he is. During a Christmastime speech to the troops in 2018, Trump bragged how the troops had not received a raise in more than 10 years (not close to being true by the way), but *"I got you a big one."* Trump, the apparent savior president and knight-in-shining-armor to the military, went on to infer that the soldiers he was speaking to would receive a 10% or greater pay raise[17]. This also was false. The base pay increase for the 10-years prior to President Trump averaged 2.1% per year (not zero), and the base pay increase in 2019 was nowhere near 10%[18]. It was 2.6%.

OK, you may think to yourself... well 2.6% is still better than the average increase over the last decade so this is an improvement, right? No, not really. Recall that the last 10 years included what is considered the second-worst economic downturn in U.S. economic history, so it would make sense that the nation would have to be tight on pay increases as it needed to stop the bleeding.

More telling though, is a comparison of the base pay increase rates to the COLA rates. The 'cost-of-living-adjustments' (COLA) are calculated by the Social Security administration to account for increases to the cost-of-living each year. When you compare the difference between the raise rates and the COLA rates over time, this accounts for

[17] https://time.com/5489492/trump-military-raise/

[18] https://www.militarytimes.com/pay-benefits/military-pay-center/2019/01/03/the-new-pay-raise-is-in-effect-heres-the-2019-basic-pay-chart/

the change to actual buying power due to the pay increases in question.

Base salary increases during the Trump administration average 0.2% over COLA. Rate increases during Obama's administration averaged 0.59% over COLA – almost three times more than during the Trump administration[19]. In short, Trump is not improving the situation for the military with regards to base pay when you take the bigger picture into account. To date, he is significantly worse than his predecessor.

In December 2017, Trump signed the Tax Cuts and Jobs Act (TCJA), a plan that made significant changes to federal tax policy. Although many household's federal tax rates were lowered, including those of the average military family, the clear result of this law is that more money will rise towards the people who have most of it already, as those in the upper tax brackets will tend to benefit the most by it. For example, a family filing a married-joint-return earning $466,950 or more sees their top tax bracket decrease by 7% (from 40% to 33%), while a similar family earning $75,000 or less sees their top tax bracket decrease by only 3% (from 15% to 12%). A March 2019 article in the Atlantic[20] highlights a 2018 'Blue Star Families' report that "military families report difficulty making ends meet at twice the rate of civilian families." This being the case, it would be understandable for some of these families to feel they are given scraps while others feast.

[19] https://www.ssa.gov/oact/cola/colaseries.html

[20] https://www.theatlantic.com/family/archive/2019/03/majority-military-spouses-are-underemployed/585586/

Other items worthy of note include the following.
(1) The tax plan also included effective tax increases specific to 'Gold Star' families (families that lost a loved one in the military) as is discussed in an April 26, 2019 CNN article[21].

(2) Most of the tax cuts that could benefit many military families are set to automatically expire in 2025, while some of the tax cuts that benefit the upper end of the economic scale in the country have no expiration date.

(3) The tax cuts will have an impact on the spending ability of the country. Many programs, including those that may benefit military families, may need to be cut or sacrificed altogether as a result.

- Is Trump keeping his promise about the V.A.? –

Well, at least he is taking care of the veterans at the Veteran's Administration (V.A.), right? Wrong. *The Washington Examiner* – a conservative publication that as I write this has a huge banner advertisement on its website paid for by the 'Trump Make America Great Again Committee' – ran an op ed on May 13, 2019 with the title, *"Trump administration breaks campaign promise, purges 200,000 VA healthcare applications"*[22]. Scott Davis, the author of the piece and someone who was instrumental in bringing problems with the V.A. to light during Obama's administration, writes:

---

[21] https://www.cnn.com/2019/04/26/politics/military-families-tax-change-trump/index.html

[22] https://www.washingtonexaminer.com/opinion/op-eds/trump-administration-breaks-campaign-promise-purges-200-000-va-healthcare-applications

"But after two years in the White House, the Trump administration has decided to execute a plan to purge 200,000 applications for VA healthcare caused by known administrative errors within VA's enrollment process and enrollment system — problems that had already been documented by the Office of the Inspector General in 2015 and 2017.

In purging this massive backlog of applications, the VA is declaring the applications to be incomplete due to errors by the applicants, despite the OIG findings and in violation of the promise Trump made to fix the system. This purge has the dual effect of letting the VA avoid the work of processing the applications and absolving the agency of any responsibility for veterans' delayed access to health and disability benefits....

As a result, to win benefits wrongfully denied due to VA's administrative errors, veterans are forced to go to court and pay legal fees out of whatever benefits they ultimately win."

The moral importance of tending to the well-being of our veterans should be clear, especially during a time when the suicide rate is twice as high among veterans than among non-veteran citizens. Trump appears to care much less about this than he did on the 2016 campaign trail.

- Other Military and Security Concerns –

I'd imagine that if I was active military or had direct family in the military, I would be running constant calculations in the back of my head regarding the likelihood of deployment to war. I am not military, and I have a low-grade stress level about these concerns for the country as it is. Donald Trump's instability terrifies me. It is clear that he is winging it.

(1) He is willfully providing state-of-the-art weaponry and potentially nuclear technology to Saudi Arabia's murderous regime. Do you really think that is a good thing long term? Recall that the U.S. helped support the Afghan resistance in the Soviet-Afghan war in the 1980's. One of the indirect beneficiaries was a young Osama bin Laden, and the long-view on that one did not turn out well for us. (I do know there are layers of complexity related to that war and I do not mean to oversimplify it. My only point is that we need to be careful who we support.)

(2) He overturns the disallowance of security clearances, including to his son-in-law, Jared Kushner. Kushner was said publicly to have had his clearance revoked, but then apparently had it reinstated later by the urging (or order) of the president. Recall that the Mueller Report indicated that Russia saw Kushner as a potential target to get them prized information about the administration.

(3) Trump's cozying up to Putin and his ongoing, public lover's quarrels with Kim Jong-un do nothing to calm the nerves. I wouldn't put it past Putin or Jong-un to take action that could lead to a war response.

(4) It appears that those military personnel in Trumps' orbit do not think highly of him at all. Consider this from the November 16, 2018 New York Times[23]:

"There was the belief that over time, he would better understand, but I don't know that that's the case," said Col. David Lapan, a retired Marine who served in the Trump administration in 2017 as a spokesman for the Department of Homeland Security. "I don't think that he understands the proper use and role of the military and what we can, and can't, do."

(5) Trump also seems to use the military for political purposes. To hell with strategic preparation or tactical military training. It appears the Trump administration has much more important missions in mind... for example, ordering the military to paint some of the existing southern border wall primarily for aesthetic purposes[24].

Oh, that's right. I remember now from all those campaign rallies:

"Paint the Wall! Paint the Wall! Paint the Wall!..."

My Ask:

In summary, Trump lied about the raises that would be going to the military, and the raises that did eventually get implemented represent a third of the net benefit that was provided under the average Obama administration pay scale. He has broken a big campaign promise regarding improvement to the Veterans Administration and approved what effectively is a tax hike on Gold Star families. His tax plan will likely help military families far less than those who

[23] https://www.nytimes.com/2018/11/16/us/politics/president-trump-military.html

[24] https://slate.com/news-and-politics/2019/06/trump-military-deployment-paint-one-mile-border-wall.html

typically have higher family incomes. He provides military technology to murderous regimes, has essentially been called out as an idiot by military staff, discards standard protocol regarding our nation's secrets, and is directing military focus (and funding) to the color choice of paint on a fence.

My ask for this section is that you – like me – vomit the next time you see Trump hug an American flag in front of soldiers.

08. "Trump will be good for the economy."

Of all the claims Trump made during his campaign, one of the most frequent was that he would be the economic savior for the country. He claimed the economy was going to hell in a handbasket (which it clearly was not), and that only he could save the day. Despite his multiple corporate bankruptcies (see the "Trump is an excellent businessman" section), many found him convincing and believed that he would indeed be good for the economy.

2019 Update:

Since his election, Trump takes any chance he can get to flaunt that the U.S. economy is doing great and how quickly he "turned things around." The economy, as it turns out though, is like any complicated system, in that it is, well... complicated. If there was a simple and immediate on-off switch for economic success, which politician would refuse it? Let's get past the "best ever" claims from Trump, and actually look in some level of detail at how common economic indicators have trended during the Trump administration so far.

- Stock Market -

August 22, 2018 was a busy day for Trump on Twitter. He had comments to make about his respect for his campaign chair and (newly-convicted criminal) Paul Manafort, he gave a shout-out to @foxandfriends to publicize his pending interview there, he bragged again about an election he had won almost two years prior to "Crooked Hillary", he slammed his personal lawyer for years Michael Cohen (after

Cohen pleaded guilty in court and connected Trump to potential crimes), and of course... Witch Hunt!

With all that activity, Trump was still somehow able to sneak in a tweet about the economy: *"Longest bull run in the history of the stock market, congratulations America!"*

I am happy to see that he did not directly claim credit for this run (in this tweet at least), but two days later, he seemed to roll this record right under the "Excellent Trump Economy" umbrella in another tweet: *"Our Economy is setting records on virtually every front – Probably the best our country has ever done. Tremendous value created since the Election. The World is respecting us again! Companies are moving back to the U.S.A."*

It is true that Trump's administration coincides with the longest "bull market" in the country's history, but it is important to point out that this longest bull market actually started on March 9, 2009. This change from bear-to-bull occurred only two months into the Obama administration and it stayed a bull market for Obama's whole presidency.

I rarely credit or blame a president for the well-being of the economy during their administration simply because there are so many factors outside of their control that affect the economy. In the case of Obama, however, I (and many economists) believe he mostly pulled the right levers that were within his reach. I think he correctly controlled what he could control. The next time Trump parades the "longest bull market" through social media, just remember that 75% of it occurred on Obama's watch.

- Jobs -

Trump also loves to talk about how he is bringing jobs back to the country. He gleefully talks about pressuring heads of companies (such as General Motors) to bring jobs back. If any of you reading this voted for Trump because he would "keep government out of business," were you not also alarmed by Trumps' actions? So much for the laissez-faire ideology in the Republican Party I guess?

There are two incredibly useful graphics that detail U.S. job growth. The first one [25] (see below) is by economist Aaron Sojourner from the University of Minnesota's Carlson School of Management and it eviscerates any notion that Trump is an honest broker on the topic.

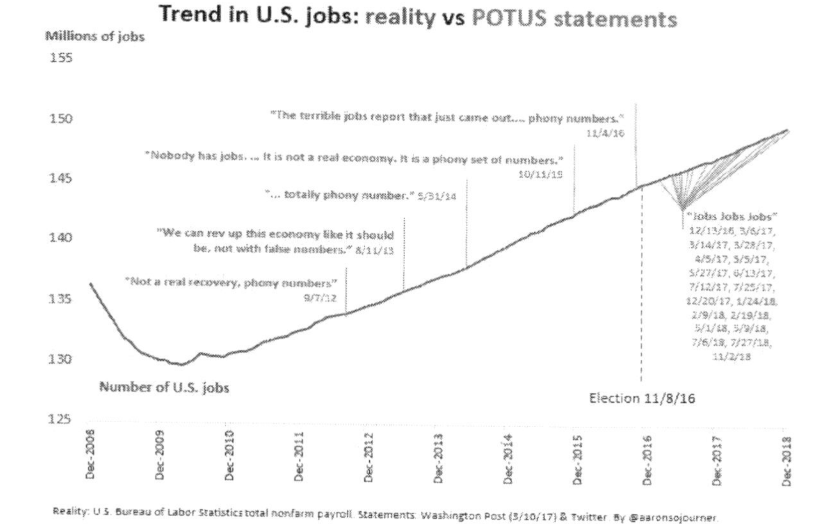

[25] https://twitter.com/aaronsojourner/status/1089880090949898243

It shows consistent job growth since 2010. When this occurred during Obama's administration, Trump claimed that the job numbers were "phony" or "false." The second he took over, the numbers magically turned 'great' and he wouldn't shut up about them – even though the slope of the job growth line was essentially the same as it had been since 2010.

The other graphic[26] is from propublica.org and is an interactive tool. It tracks jobs Trump has promised (hint: it was a lot – 8,900,000) vs jobs in reality that hiring companies attribute to Trump policies (hint: it is NOT a lot -- 797).

Also, very noticeable in the graphic is the 1,000,000 jobs that Jack Ma (head of the Chinese company, Alibaba) promised to help develop in the United States. Ma later revoked his promise due to Trump's anti-China stance, indicating that his initial promise was based on an understanding of a "friendly U.S.-China partnership," an understanding that later appeared misguided in light of Trump's stances on tariffs.

- Gross Domestic Product –

If you have never seen or read it, I highly recommend Robert Kennedy's March 18, 1968 speech[27] concerning the Gross Domestic Product (GDP). It is short, but still effective in getting me to question the metrics we use to grade

---

[26] https://projects.propublica.org/graphics/trump-job-promises
[27] https://www.theguardian.com/news/datablog/2012/may/24/robert-kennedy-gdp

ourselves as a country. That said, the GDP is still a common metric used to gauge the economy so let's look at it.

In 2018, the increase in GDP from the previous year was 2.9%[28]. Receiving this news, Trump tweeted *"GDP growth during the four quarters of 2018 was the fastest since 2005."* This is some REAL wordsmithing here. GDP growth in 2005 was 3.5% and the next fastest GDP since 2005 is indeed 2.9%, so you could argue that Trump did not technically lie when he tweeted what he did. It is very obvious though that he was purposefully being misleading, as GDP growth of 2.9% was also recorded in 2015, the year immediately before he was elected.

Like the economy in general, there are so many factors outside presidential control that impact the GDP that it really is unfair to pin these numbers on the presidents. For the record, the average GDP annual growth for each of the last presidential administrations going back to Carter are as follows: Carter (2.6%), Reagan (3.5%), George HW Bush (2.3%), B. Clinton (3.8%), George W Bush (2.2%), Obama (1.6%), Trump to-date (2.6%). Regarding things outside of presidential control, consider things like the development of the internet (Clinton), 9/11 (George W Bush), inheriting the "Great Recession" and "sequestration" by Congress (Obama). In light of all this, Trump at 2.6% is truly nothing remarkable, especially since he inherited a relatively stable economy and economists are building consensus that signs now point to an economic downturn in the near future.

- National Debt -

[28] https://www.thebalance.com/us-gdp-by-year-3305543

Do you remember the days when Republicans would talk about the growing national debt as if it meant something? I do. It was three years ago, when a non-Republican was in office. Now Trump is there, and... crickets.

One of my biggest anxieties with far-left platforms is the apparent nonconcern whatsoever about the growing national debt. My anxiety is now also shared about head-in-the-sand Republicans. The American Recovery and Reinvestment Act (ARRA) of 2009, viewed by many as the necessary piece of legislation that walked the U.S. economy back from the cliff, also had a very noteworthy and negative impact on the national debt. Trump was all over this on Twitter during Obama's presidency. Now that the deficit is up another ~$2.5 trillion since he's been in office... again, crickets.

- Other Economic Considerations –

I have already touched a few times on not tying a president too closely to the national economy that happens to exist at the time of her or his administration. That said, there are clearly things that Trump and like-minded folks in Congress are doing that I think are economically dangerous, unsustainable, or both.

(1) The Trump Tax plan in 2017 clearly favors those living in the upper portion of the economic spectrum. I am not convinced that spurring an even greater wealth gap is good for the long-term health or security of the nation. Furthermore, the projected earnings from the tax plan are expected to drop significantly for these last two years of the

first Trump term, resulting in some economists referring to the plan as a "sugar high"[29] (a term used by JP Morgan).

(2) Trump's love of tariffs seems to have a destabilizing effect on the national and global economy. Referring to himself as "Tariff Man" in a December 2018 tweet, Trump goes on to say he wants *"people or countries (who) come in to raid the great wealth of our Nation... to pay for the privilege of doing so."* It does not appear that he understands that the American consumer typically ends up paying for the cost increase of tariffs, not the "raiders."

I get the long-term argument... that tariffs raise prices on foreign goods and then make non-foreign goods more attractive to the American consumer. But now American companies are operating with less competition, which may sound good on the surface until you realize that less competition usually means companies can raise prices... and the American consumer having to pay more again, may just go back to the foreign product anyway.

But at least the American companies are making more money for a little while, right? OK, sounds good... until you recognize that trade wars are not one-sided. Other countries retaliate (similar to China right now) and increase tariffs on American products coming in through their borders, making them more expensive and less attractive to their citizens.

Businesses are always looking for the next customer base, and guess what... there are many more potential

---

[29] https://www.axios.com/end-sugar-rush-tax-reform-212b820c-bcc6-429e-894c-17a3894edb51.html

customers outside the United States than inside it. The U.S. at 327 million people is only 4.3% of the world's 7.53 billion population. With purchasing power in some of these countries increasing significantly – including in the most populous country, China – U.S. companies may be priced out of those markets. Fortunately, even Republicans worked to talk Trump back from the "trade war" ledge in June 2019, after he had announced his plan to put tariffs on products from Mexico.

(3) Trump has been eager to trash regulations on businesses in the country. The argument is that other countries do not have to deal with some of these regulations and therefore, they create a disadvantage for the American business in the global marketplace. This makes sense and I am for it... for those regulations that really are outdated or counterproductive. I am not for blind deregulation, however, and Trump does not seem to distinguish between a smart or dumb regulation.

Keep in mind that the repeal in 1999 of the Glass-Steagall Act of 1933 is typically considered a primary cause[30] of the painful 2008 recession. In the rush to deregulate, Trump may be planting the seeds for the next big financial crisis.

It is also worthy of note that Republicans did not always view the regulation of business as a bad thing. After all, the Environmental Protection Agency (EPA) – a frequent target of attack for Trump supporters – was created under Republican President Nixon.

---

[30] https://www.thebalance.com/what-caused-2008-global-financial-crisis-3306176

(4) Trump likes to put pressure on the Federal Reserve Chairperson (currently Jerome Powell) to refrain from raising interest rates. Although the Reserve is supposed to be independent of presidential influence, most presidents have had far more respect for the importance of that independence than our current president does. As the economy grows stronger, the fed typically raises interest rates. In the event of a crash in the future, the fed can then lower rates as a means to help re-stimulate the economy. When that lever is already on the floor, the power of this economic weapon is depleted. Breaking the glass to pull the fire alarm does no good when the alarm is dead.

(5) Perhaps most importantly, Trump is looking backwards. With his focus on bringing manufacturing back to the United States, he is convinced that things will be like they were before. He envisions a bunch of new U.S. manufacturing jobs that people will slave over, and all will be good again in the world. He completely seems to miss that this is not the same world it was in the 1950's. The industrial revolution is often talked about in history books as if it ended. It has not. Technology continues to replace all sorts of jobs. Yes, people are still currently needed to work in manufacturing plants, but there are far less seats at the table for these jobs now than decades ago.

Technology has improved to the point where developments in robotics, artificial intelligence (AI), and machine learning (ML) may be nearing a tipping point when replacement of people in the workplace will explode even further upwards, affecting both blue and white-collar jobs alike. Trump can continue to blame it on jobs going to

Mexico and China, but when people start to recognize just how powerful AI is becoming, this will soon by an irrelevant point. To be clear, this admittedly is not just a Trump problem. I don't get the sense that many of the people running for President in 2020 understand this issue like they should.

The trucking industry (and pending changes to it) is another example of technology's likely game-changing impact. "Truck driver" is currently the most common job in over half of the states in the country (and RTS Financial[31] indicates that 7.4 million American jobs relate to the truck-driving industry), yet self-driving technology is here right now as an existential threat. Is Trump taking this seriously? Apparently not. Instead he reportedly refers to vehicles with this technology as *"crazy driverless cars"* and supposedly told a Tesla driver *"I don't trust some computer to drive me around."* In the meantime, Trump's own Department of Transportation has recognized that a "new era of transportation innovation"[32] is upon us.

As exciting new opportunities arise in the renewable energy industry, Trump is still talking about the importance of coal as an energy source. I can't help but think that leaders of other countries are developing "0-to-60-mph in 1 second," electric, self-driving Lamborghinis, while Trump is riding a dying donkey, whipping it to go faster. He seems to have almost no vision and no ability to "see-around-the-corner" when it comes to what the future is likely to be. I

[31] https://www.rtsfinancial.com/articles/why-trucking-still-america-s-number-one-job
[32] https://www.transportation.gov/AV

suppose this could be expected from someone who still refuses to use "the computer."

<u>My Ask</u>:

My asks for this section are that you please recognize the following.

(1) When Trump brags about the economy, he does so having been the beneficiary of a pre-existing upswing in the economic cycle.

(2) The "Trump economy," despite what he shouts from the mountaintops... and Twitter, is not that special when compared to economies during prior administrations.

(3) Although there are many impacts to an economic cycle that occur independent of a presidency, the economy-impacting actions that Trump has taken so far are dangerously risky and likely unsustainable.

(4) There are real limitations to the metrics we use to measure the well-being of the economy at large. As Robert Kennedy said, the GDP "*can tell us everything about America except why we are proud that we are Americans.*" The stock market also is limiting as a gauge. With income inequality in the country being as it currently is, it would be wrong to assume that a rising stock market automatically improves everyone's economic standing.

(5) Finally, Trump truly seems to lack an understanding of how technology is changing the world economy (and how it impacts jobs).

09. "I'm sticking with the home team (Republicans)."

S.E. Cupp, a Republican pundit and former Trump friend said something in 2016 that stuck out to me as likely prescient when she said it. I did not find the transcript so I may be off a word or two, but she said something along the lines of: *"The Republican Party can survive a Trump candidacy, but it cannot survive a Trump presidency."* I was impressed with her and a handful of other Republicans who consistently spoke out against Trump and the danger he could pose to the country. Many, however, jumped on the Trump train when he won the nomination.

2019 Update:

Since taking office, I have been sickened by the amount of people that continue to make excuses for President Trump. I understand the whole argument that people are too politically correct and Trump is attacked just because he is not "PC." But come on… come on people! I am not going to take the time to go through everything that Trump has said or done to embarrass us as a country or every time he has said or done completely unnecessary things that have caused people real pain. It might literally take years to even attempt doing justice to such a thing. Just look back at the "Trump tells-it-like-it-is" section and click on the link that documents his false or misleading statements. How people can still defend this man is beyond my understanding.

Even this morning as I sat down to write this (June 9, 2019), I came across reporting that Fox News anchor Laura Ingraham called out something Trump said as "fake news." I was of course surprised by this, so I looked further.

Ingraham looks directly at the camera and says the following:

> *"Some of you may have heard or read that president Trump supposedly held up the entire D-Day ceremony in order to do this interview with me. That is patently false... fake news."* (Reference the 4:13 mark in the CNN video on YouTube, entitled: "Watch Fox News host call Trump statement 'fake news'"[33]).

OK, but the inference she is making here is that of course once again the crazy, lefty fake-news media is responsible for this misunderstanding, yet when you go see the actual interview she had with Trump, you see this is not the case. Trump's own words are as follows:

> *"Listen to those incredible people back there. These people are so amazing and what they don't realize is that I'm holding them up because of this interview but that's because it's you... by the way, congratulations on your ratings, I've very proud of you."*

I thought that this may be taken out of context and perhaps he was being sarcastic, but no... it certainly doesn't seem that way to me (see the 11:07 point on the realclearpolitics.com[34] link to see for yourself.)

On the grand scheme of things, this I'm sure seems like a small, small thing, but I don't think it is. It helps prove the

[33] https://www.youtube.com/watch?v=e2ATRw_P_ik

[34] https://www.realclearpolitics.com/video/2019/06/06/full_trump_interview_with_laura_ingraham_democrats_have_been_going_after_me_and_they_have_nothing.html

point I am making. Here is a scenario where a clear Trump-sycophant feels the need to correct the record for something that happened during her own interview. Even though Trump himself is obviously to blame for the misunderstanding, she cannot bring herself to admit it. Instead she takes a stance that protects Trump from his own words, implying yet again that the crazy news media are at it again.

People are sticking with their home team GOP, even when the current GOP (and country's) leader is saying and doing things that are embarrassingly childish. What is more surprising to me though is that many GOP-homebodies seem to be fine with staying with the home team, even when their leader is undercutting things that they have claimed to believe for years. These includes the following.

(1) The GOP appears to have undergone a near-full-reversal in how it views Russia. Russia was a clear threat, and then the GOP platform softened towards Russia considerably with the Trump GOP nomination, which modified language regarding support for the Ukraine. There are now even Trump supporter that wear "I'd Rather be a Russian than a Democrat" tee-shirts. This is happening, mind you, even when we have full consensus from all our intelligence agencies that Russia is systematically attempting to weaken our democratic system. So much for patriotism I guess.

(2) The GOP has shifted significantly since Trump took over regarding its perspective on free and open trade (which you'd think would be a clear benchmark for any capitalistic

system). People forget that although NAFTA (North American Free Trade Agreement) was signed into law by President Clinton in 1993, it had more Republican support than Democratic support in Congress. Now, with Trump, it is suddenly the worse thing ever.

Also, Republicans were never fans of tariffs, but since Trump, GOP-support for them has increased significantly. In early June 2019, Trump threatened tariffs against Mexico and thankfully there does seem to be real GOP-pushback against that (and in fairness, there has been some GOP-pushback against pulling out of NAFTA too), but Trump has nonetheless clearly pulled the GOP towards his position on the matter.

(3) The GOP has seemingly taken its eye off the "financial-responsibility" ball. As discussed previously, GOP calls to attack the national debt have gone all but silent. The swing towards tariffs just mentioned is also typically viewed by economists as a big mistake economically.

(4) The GOP has shifted on immigration. Trump had made immigration such a huge issue in his 2016 campaign that I considered making this one of the 15 specific reasons noted in this book. I chose not to do so in large part because there is already so much coverage on this topic. During the campaign, the "*Build the Wall*" chants were endless. Trump referred to the wall-to-be as being "*made of hardened concrete"... "no windows, no nothing – precast concrete going very high"*[35] and of course, Mexico was going to pay

[35] https://www.npr.org/2019/01/11/683920624/once-a-fence-later-slats-almost-always-a-wall-trumps-border-wall-contradictions

for it. This obviously has not happened, but in truth, I think the Trump administration has done exactly what some would have expected him to do on this topic since taking over.

Trump is doing what he can to scrounge for funding to use on his pet wall project, including military funding as discussed earlier. There are frequent concerns raised about the treatment of those immigrants who are detained, but in truth, it really appears that many Trump voters simply don't care about these conditions... or more accurately, they don't care enough to allow those conditions to force a reconsideration of their 2020 vote.

It is understandable that someone who might not have been paying close attention would believe that the GOP has always been hard on immigration into the United States. I do recall hearing "no amnesty" for those people illegally in the country as a GOP rallying cry for some time. This, however, was always only part of the GOP perspective.

There was also a much more measured and reasonable approach to the issue not that long ago and it had a real voice in the GOP. Recently passed Senator John McCain was an example of this. He called for a comprehensive immigration reform that flew in the face of the present-day hardline and Trump-led mentality. In his 2018 memoir entitled, "The Restless Wave: Good Times, Just Causes, Great Fights and Other Appreciations," McCain (with co-author Mark Salter) wrote about the immigration debate:

"We failed twice, and then once more after Ted (Kennedy) had passed away, despite big majorities in both houses of Congress in favor of it... I'd like to say I'll try again. But that is not up to me anymore. That's a harder disappointment than other defeats have been because first, it's something that most Americans want, and most members of Congress know is the right thing to do."

Instead, much of the GOP has been stuck fixating on construction of additional border wall that, although potentially helpful to a small degree, is a red herring of momentous proportions. Of course, additional barrier might help stem some illegal immigration and we can look into that, but there appear to be much more effective tools at our disposal and much better uses of our money to reach our stated goal. The most reasoned summary I have seen in response to Trump's obsession with building additional walls along the southern border comes from Congressman Scott Peters from San Diego. At 3:05 in a "Democratic Weekly Address" video[36] on House Speaker Nancy Pelosi's Facebook page, Peters makes the very important point that:

"If Homeland Security wanted to recommend something as expensive as a wall in a particular place, they'd have to justify the extra expense against other less costly tools."

Technologies to detect tunnels and/or sensors and radar on camera-equipped drones appear to give us much better bang for the buck.

---

[36] https://www.facebook.com/NancyPelosi/videos/764702923888006/?v=764702923888006

And just for fun, I recommend the GOP members who see themselves as "immigration hardliners" take a look at Republican god Ronald Reagan and (admittedly, not quite a Republican-god) George H.W. Bush fight over themselves in a 1980 debate[37] to show who can be more sensitive and decent to immigrants from Mexico. Reagan is even quoted as saying *"open the border both ways."*

My Ask:

There has been much made of how "modern tribalism" has affected our society and political discourse. We have picked a team and we no longer think beyond that. If the team goes one way, we go that way. If it goes the other way, we go the other way. The other side is demonized.

At times, though, like-minded people that you may respect will sometimes break away from the group a bit on a given issue, and this causes discomfort. The ground is splitting underneath your feet and you need to make a decision. On what piece of ground will you stand? Will you go with the person you respect or stay with the safety of your crowd? What if 10% of your group follows that person? Or 20%... or 30%? Where will you go to seek solid ground? At what point do you leave the group behind?

These "tribal tremors" are not welcomed by those with the group-think mentality, but I am convinced that they are absolutely necessary – even for our survival as a species. (I get that may sound overly dramatic, but I do not think it is. If

---

[37] https://www.usatoday.com/videos/news/2017/01/28/george-h.-w.-bush-and-ronald-reagan-debate-immigration-1980/97184364/

you are interested, feel free to read something else I wrote back in July 2016, entitled "Joining the Tribe"[38].)

I ask that you rid yourself of the "right vs left" mentality and snap out of the "hippies vs squares" psychological loop that this country has been in since the 1960's. The world has changed. We need to adapt to how the world is now and take steps to make it how we want it to be in the future. Let's address the issues one-by-one as they need to be addressed. To "both sides," please stop thinking how "your group" tells you to think. Think for yourself.

To GOP'ers, I ask that you be open to the reality of President Trump as the leader of your party and that you see how he is changing it. If there is ever a time to be receptive to tribal tremors, it is now. Trump, indeed, is an earthquake... and earthquakes do not play favorites. They can – and do – take down lefties and righties alike.

[38] https://medium.com/@stevedowpe/joining-the-tribe-e7d44854126b

10. "The other side is much worse."

One of the most common reasons I heard from Trump voters for voting for Trump in 2016 was that they simply never would vote for Hillary Clinton. The "lesser of two evils" argument was made all the time and I grew bored of it quickly. To me, it was a symptom of people being lazy... not wanting to (a) do the real research into who Trump was, (b) be honest with themselves about who Trump was, and/or (c) leave the comfort of their political tribe as we just discussed. I was not a huge Hillary Clinton fan, but it was not a "lesser of two evils" situation for me. I saw it as a serious (albeit flawed) politician vs an absolute nightmare of a conman.

2019 Update:

I'd like to do an "update" since the 2016 election here, but apparently there may not be much need. It turns out that the 2016 election is still current news for President Trump. Today (June 9, 2019) is 943 days after the 2016 election, and even today, Trump is re-tweeting about his "historic landslide election." Recall that it was not a landslide by the way, and he actually lost the popular vote by approximately 3 million votes... I'd say "who cares" at this point... but Trump clearly still does.

- Still Human –

Yesterday, I watched a 2016 episode of the Netflix show "Black Mirror" with my son entitled "Men Against Fire." SPOILER ALERT: The episode is about futuristic soldiers who have had their brains conditioned to see a targeted group of people as subhuman. Whereas normal people would see this targeted group as other human beings, the soldiers would physically see "roaches," a subhuman animal (that looked very much like vampires in science fiction or horror movies). This is done to make it psychologically easier for the soldiers to kill these targets. END SPOILER ALERT.

Such talk of "subhumans" may make sense in future dystopian stories, but sadly, this subjugation of others to a subhuman level also fills our history books. And yes, it exists in multiple places throughout the world today. One place I had hoped not to see it was in American politics, but it is there as well. In June 2017, President Trump's son Eric made an appearance on Fox News, telling entertainer Sean Hannity what he feels about some of his father's political opposition: *"to me, they're not even people."*

Talk like this really makes me want to find some way to get people to pause, take a step back, take a deep breath in... then slowly exhale. All that endless anger that gets people spun up by watching Tucker Carson.... all that exhausted exacerbation of nerves people get while watching Rachel Maddow simply report the daily absurdities ... all of it... let it go... exhale... ex....haaaaaaaaaallllllllleee. We are all people. We all have flaws. It is true that some of us are real jerks or even psychopaths, but I believe the vast majority of us want good for ourselves, our families, and the world in general. We need to be able keep that as our starting point.

- Those Radical Socialists... -

It is true that the Democratic party does have a more recent push towards what some call the "far left." Thanks in large part to Bernie Sanders, the term "socialism" has arisen from the basement of taboo words, only to be shot continually with arrows and demonized further as "radicalism run amuck." It clearly is the boogeyman word Trump is already starting to parade as red meat in front of his base for 2020. It is chapter #1 in the 2020 "The Other Side is Worse" Trump playbook, so let's further address it here.

What often seems lost on people is that there are varying degrees of socialism, just as there are varying degrees of capitalism. Not many conservatives would say they are against government ownership of national parks or that they are against reasonable regulations on corporations (such as those that exist to guard against monopoly), but this does not make them socialists. Likewise, many liberals may be wary of certain characteristics inherent in capitalism that many conservatives don't seem to sweat, but this doesn't mean that they are necessarily looking to throw out the "capitalism baby" with the bath water. The debate should be about where to find the balance. It should not be a debate on strawman arguments that only some on the very far extremes are making.

I remember being proud of something I wrote in a term paper for one of my favorite MBA classes (a business ethics course) in 2003:

> *"Capitalism is a wild horse, powerful and fast, but also dangerous... just as a horse is only useful to the rider when it can be ridden, capitalism is only useful to society when its self-destructive tendencies can be tempered."*

Whereas a horse may come with a saddle, bit, and reigns, it makes sense that a capitalistic system may come with regulations, restrictions, and reporting requirements. Without some level of control, people get trampled underfoot.

The flip side is true as well. Socialism may be only useful when some of its potentially "motivation-killing" tendencies are counter-balanced. After all, too much control can be a bad thing. Keeping a powerful horse locked in a cage, for example, doesn't serve a purpose for anyone.

Adam Smith, the "patron saint of capitalism," wrote what is essentially the capitalists' Bible, *The Wealth of Nations* in 1776. In it, he lays out the theory of capital markets, division of labor, and supply and demand. What many do not mention is that this book also highlights negative aspects of capitalism that work against the public good and ought to be addressed. Again, he hints at finding the proper balance.

My Ask:

I ask that you stop the demonization of others that don't think like you. When you find yourself defaulting immediately to "the other side is much worse," step back out of the spin cycle and listen to the heart of what is being proposed.

Perhaps some of it will strike you as nonsense (and some of it indeed may be), but much of it is not. Maybe it truly is a radical departure from your thinking, but that doesn't make it wrong or unworthy of review. Much of what is proposed is suitable for serious policy discussion. We should respect that and give it our real attention and consideration. I ask that we stop throwing bombs and we listen. I ask for the return of a respectful and civil discourse.

11. "A Clinton presidency would be mired in controversy."

The argument was that (despite the FBI's review and final reporting clearing her on the issue), Hillary Clinton's deleted emails were going to haunt the country for her entire presidency. The 10+ investigations and 10+ hours of Hillary Clinton testifying directly before Congress about Benghazi was not enough and this also would live on during her presidency. Did we as a nation really want to elect someone who – whether she was innocent or guilty – would result in the country being embroiled in political drama for years? It would stall any progress.

We as a country simply need to move on, right?

2019 Update:
WRONG. Bigly Wrong! We are not moving on, but this fact has very little to do with Hillary Clinton.

It is absolutely painful to think about writing out all of the scandals and controversies associated with Donald Trump. A March 24, 2019 *Time Magazine* article [39] came out almost a month before the redacted version of the Mueller Report was made public, but it still captures a good chunk of the controversies surrounding Trump. It is certainly worth the read.

Perhaps you don't mind Trump's dangerous brinkmanship style in both national and global politics, his

[39] https://time.com/5557644/donald-trump-other-investigations-mueller/

record-setting staff turnover rate, his tendency to refer to the free press as the "enemy of the people," or that he appoints people to positions for which they are wholly unqualified. Maybe you are not perturbed that he lies to the American people at an almost superhuman rate, while he hides behind his lawyers when it comes to testifying under oath. I can envision a scene in a movie in Trump's head, where he is explaining how he wants to testify under oath:

> *"Hold me back... hold me back... I really really want to testify but my lawyers say no...so... otherwise, oh boy.. Would I testify? ... I'd testify BIGLY... HUGELY... I'd be the best testifier ever... you know the Terminator? They'd call me the Testifier... if only I could make my own decision to testify... I would be tremendous... I would be great... but you know... lawyers..."*

Perhaps you are not phased that our president may have to postpone answering the proverbial "emergency 3 a.m. phone call" until he finishes his Twitter battle with Bette Midler. Maybe you don't care that he is historically slow in nominating candidates for certain governmental positions (whether it be by purposeful intention or ineptitude). I am concerned about all of these things, but in the interest of eventually ending this section, I need to choose among the available controversies.

- Non-Mueller-Report Stuff –

(1) Possible violations of the Emoluments Clause (Article 1, Section 9, Clause 8 of the U.S. Constitution).

I've already touched on some of these concerns and how they specifically relate to Saudi Arabia in the "Trump will defend us & be tough on our adversaries" section. A December 6, 2018 *Vanity Fair* article [40] and the *Washington Post* article on which it is partially based both highlight key details. For those of you who default to questioning "liberal media" such as these two publications, I simply ask that you indicate which facts in the articles are incorrect.

(2) Status as an unindicted co-conspirator in the Stormy Daniels affair and "hush money" case.

Michael Cohen was found guilty and is in jail now in large part due to criminal activity related to the Stormy Daniels hush-money case. Cohen testified that payments to Daniels were made at the direction of a "candidate for federal office." Although he did not initially name Trump by name, he certainly was not talking about Ted Cruz. Cohen later provided checks from Trump that he said were reimbursement checks related to the payoff.

If Trump was not currently president, it is all but certain that he would be charged as a "co-conspirator" to this crime. Current Justice Department policy guidance that sitting presidents ought not be charged with a crime essentially makes Trump an "unindicted co-conspirator" right now. With Cohen currently in jail, and in light of the evidence that Trump directed the crime, it would follow that, under any other circumstance, Trump would be serving jail time right now as well.

---

[40] https://www.vanityfair.com/news/2018/12/trump-hotel-saudi-arabia

As a quick aside, Trump had told the American people that he didn't know anything about the affair allegations. This was a demonstrable lie, as there is audio evidence of him talking about it earlier. This affair apparently happened while Trump's wife, Melania, was pregnant with their child.

It is not my intent to focus on what most would consider to be this significant character flaw in Trump's personal life. I mention it here primarily to juxtapose it against the Bill Clinton impeachment hearings in 1998, when he was accused of lying under oath about a sexual affair. The main difference I see is that Trump to date has avoided having to testify under oath on this case.

- Mueller Report Stuff –

I write now on June 10, 2019 and just for fun, I made a mental bet with myself that Trump tweeted again today that there was "No Collusion! No Obstruction!" Just checked, and yep, I won! He did. I don't remember too much from my high school Shakespeare class, but he "*doth protest too much*" (from Hamlet) keeps circling back in my head. I've downloaded and listened to the Mueller Report audiobook. I hope that everyone does that or reads the text. Here are my main take-aways:

I. Collusion with Russia –

(1) Collusion is not a legal term. Mueller had to prove that Trump willfully and actively engaged in a conspiracy with Russia to commit a crime, and the legal bar to prove conspiracy is extremely high.

(2) Mueller was able to unearth significant evidence that Trump's campaign actively sought and welcomed information that was illegally obtained by Russia.

(3) Trump's campaign chair Paul Manafort instructed that campaign polling data be shared with foreign nationals with strong ties to Russian intelligence. Rick Gates (Trumps' deputy campaign manager) did indeed share this information more than once. The expectation was that this data would find its way to a man with direct ties to Putin.

(4) Recall that both Rick Gates[41] and Paul Manafort[42] pled guilty to charges of "conspiracy against the United States." Although these charges related primarily to financial and nondisclosure crimes and might not have tied directly to Russia's attack, they do show that both Gates and Manafort were willing to commit crimes with sketchy pro-Russia foreign nationals, with whom they clearly had developed a "working" relationship. Their sudden role in the leadership of the Trump campaign certainly sticks out as a concerning development.

Recognize that every time Trump claims "no collusion" with Russia, he is conveniently skipping over the fact that key leadership in his own campaign staff did indeed conspire with pro-Russia foreigners. It is far from crazy, therefore, to think that these individuals might have leveraged their contacts oversees to commit additional conspiratorial crimes against the United States as they could relate to

[41] https://abcnews.go.com/Politics/trump-aide-rick-gates-formally-pleads-guilty-counts/story?id=53274680

[42] https://www.vox.com/2018/9/14/17860410/conspiracy-against-the-united-states-paul-manafort-plea

Russia's attack on the election. They did share polling data, after all, with pro-Russia personnel. It may just be that Mueller could not find a smoking gun specifically in Trump's hand.

(5) One reason Mueller might not have been able to find a smoking gun could be due to his finding that some of the people investigated who were:

> *"associated with the Trump Campaign deleted relevant communications or communicated during the relevant period using applications that feature encryption or that do not provide for long term retention of data or communication records..."*

Perhaps Trump can call a press conference and ask Russia (if they are listening) to see if they can find these deleted communications. It seemed to work last time.

(6) Multiple people associated with Trump who were interviewed by Mueller's team seemed to not remember information that could be very pertinent. I default to giving people the benefit of the doubt, but the quantity of lies that Trump campaign officials have been caught in condition any reasonable person to be skeptical of such claims of memory loss.

(7) Mueller was able to determine that Trump lied to the American people about his business interests in Russia. Trump may have been smart enough to stay a degree removed when possible, but the Mueller Report shows that Trump was actively lying about these business interests.

Again though, purposefully lying to the American people is not a crime... it is just a sleazy thing to do and should be completely unbecoming of a U.S. president (or presidential candidate).

II. Obstruction of Justice –

(1) There are at least ten examples in the report where there is significant evidence that Trump obstructed justice.

(2) There need not be an underlying crime for obstruction of justice to occur. Recall that although Mueller was not able to obtain enough evidence that conspiracy with Russia took place specifically in regard to the Russian attack, there were several concerning developments that at the very least hinted at the potential for such a conspiracy. It may be that there would have been sufficient evidence to charge, but for the encrypted and/or deleted data as mentioned previously. (If there truthfully is nothing to hide, it does make you wonder why Trump feels the need to obstruct these investigations as he does.)

(3) The Mueller Report lists evidence that Trump himself edited the Donald Trump Jr. statement about the "June 9, 2016 Trump Tower meeting." This may shed some light on how involved Trump gets in the details of what his underlings are doing. If he was so involved with attempting to control the story about the meeting, it would not be a stretch to believe that he may have been aware the meeting was happening in the first place.

At times, Trump seems like he floats above everyone, but when it comes to things that could threaten him personally, he seems to get involved. For this reason, it is hard to believe that he had no clue about Manafort's and Gates' criminal relationships with pro-Russia Ukrainians prior to bringing them on board to manage his campaign – especially since Trump himself had his own business history with Russia (i.e. Trump Tower Moscow, Miss Universe).

(4) Mueller made it clear that he believed Department of Justice (DOJ) policy prevented him from having the authority to charge a sitting president with a crime. He set to gather facts and present the evidence.

(5) Mueller mentioned that he did not find enough evidence to bring a conspiracy charge against Trump (see above), but regarding obstruction, Mueller stated,

"If we had had confidence that the president clearly did not commit a crime, we would have said so."

This means that Mueller found cause for concern that Trump committed a crime (or crimes).

(6) Because Mueller felt bound by DOJ policy to not charge the sitting president, he indicated that charging Trump while he is president was not even an option that he could consider.

(7) Because official charges were not an option, it followed for Mueller that the "day in court" for the president to defend himself from allegations was also not an

option while he was still president. Mueller therefore was careful to not outright say (or even heavily imply) that he thought the president was guilty. Instead, he let the facts and the evidence speak for themselves and then he specifically highlighted the constitutional means for the country to address these concerns (via Article 2, Section 4 of the U.S. Constitution, regarding presidential impeachment).

(8) Based on the above, Trump's claims that the book is closed and the "Dems just want a do-over" cannot be further from the truth. Congress now has voluminous, significant, and official DOJ evidence that Trump obstructed justice. What they do with that information is – at this point - yet to be written.

- Robert Mueller and Trump's Witch Hunt claims –

There are several placards on the wall of the "Witch Dungeon Museum" in a small town north of Boston that commemorate the town's horrible history. Placard #10 specifically caught my eye when I was there last year. It is entitled "Hanging a Policeman" and it read as follows:

> *"Constable John Willard of Salem arrested the first group of witch suspects, but a few weeks later was heard to say that it should be the accusing girls who should hang. The girls then accused him of witchcraft. He fled Salem, but was caught a week later and was hanged on August 19, 1692."*

Writing this now, I am struck by some parallels.

Robert Mueller by nearly every account had earned the respect of all Washington prior to being appointed Special Counsel. A registered Republican, Mueller received a Bronze Star and a Purple Heart for his military service during the Vietnam War. After years of service in the FBI and the DOJ, he epitomized the values that many Republicans claim to hold dear. On May 17, 2017, the former GOP Speaker of the House, Newt Gingrich, went so far as to tweet:

> *"Robert Mueller is (a) superb choice to be special counsel. His reputation is impeccable for honesty and integrity."*

Who knows if Constable John Willard back in Salem was as well-regarded, but he was obviously held in high enough esteem to hold the title of constable in the small town. He was the police officer and law enforcer in the town, and as such was tasked with investigating some of these claims of witchcraft. As he dug into the evidence, it turned out he was uncovering a picture that was in drastic contrast to the narrative that some desired. As a result, they turned on him, unleashed the dark and manic fervor that was the "Salem Witch Trials" on him, and he was sacrificed to it.

Likewise, it seems that some like Gingrich who held Mueller in such high regard initially began to speak differently of him when his evidence uncovered a story that did not coincide with what they wanted to be true. Like the townspeople of Salem, these too turned on the truth-seeker.

For all the talk of "witch hunts," Trump clearly aims to be the prime accuser in the hunt, the modern-day Abigail

Williams. All throughout the investigation, Trump would come up with any shade he could to throw at Mueller. *He left my Trump golf club on bad terms. He hired crazy liberal attorneys. He is best buds with Leakin' Jim Comey, etc, etc.* Trump certainly leads the way, but he also has lackies that do his bidding as well.

Case in point, let's look again at Newt Gingrich and his evolution on the matter. He initially spoke glowingly of Mueller, but then things started to change as crimes began to be uncovered. The following Gingrich quote appears on his Facebook page before the investigation ended:

> *"From the start, Robert Mueller's goal has been to destroy President Donald J. Trump. It has not been about justice or conducting a fair investigation. He owes it to the American people to quit this charade and shut down this so-called investigation."*

Then again after Mueller released his report, Gingrich's take on Mueller continued with this more accusatory tone. In an opinion piece on the Fox News website (June 1, 2019), Gingrich writes of Mueller:

> *"This is a clear example of a prosecutor who is trying to get an outcome regardless of evidence. In a desperate pursuit to keep the bogus Russia collusion narrative alive, Mueller is turning to Soviet-style tactics."*

Well, so much for Gingrich's take on Mueller's impeccable reputation "for honesty and integrity." If Gingrich read the actual report (which I assume he did do), he must know how damaging this report is for the president... and it is not damaging because Mueller just made up a bunch of random accusations. It is damaging because Mueller laid out a very clear and consistent trail of evidence towards the president having his hands dirty. Gingrich is going after Mueller now because the objective effort to uncover the truth does not align with the narrative Gingrich and others want to believe. Just like the Salem townspeople, he is turning on the investigator.

I see Gingrich as just one example of a Republican who has sold his soul to the cult of Trump. [This should not matter, but it is perhaps worthy of note that Trump nominated Newt's wife Callista to be the U.S. Ambassador to the Holy See (a.k.a. Vatican) in 2017. Newt converted to Catholicism after a six-year affair with Callista, a longtime Catholic.]

Many other Republicans have done this same switch on Mueller, following along with the talking points that Mueller orchestrated a modern-day witch hunt. Remember though that the biggest difference between the Russia Investigation and the Salem Witch Trials is that Mueller did indeed find some witches. In our case, real evidence led to charges being made, people admitting guilt, and people in jail.

- Post-Mueller Report and the Refusal to Govern –

I don't know what will come in the future. There is discussion now about whether articles of impeachment should be debated in Congress. With regards to the conspiracy and obstruction allegations associated with the Mueller Report, it seems certain that Congress will in one way or another pick up where Mueller felt he needed to stop.

Beyond the Mueller Report, and even beyond the many older controversies still anchored to President Trump, there is a relatively new Trump controversy that has taken the headlines of late. By encouraging (reportedly, even directing) government officials to ignore Congressional subpoenas, Trump is in dereliction of duty.

When Trump was inaugurated in January 2017, he stood before the country and swore the following oath:

> *"I, Donald John Trump, do solemnly swear that I will faithfully execute the Office of President of the United States, and will to the best of my Ability, preserve, protect and defend the Constitution of the United States."*

By encouraging people to resist Congressional subpoenas, Trump is obstructing the Congress from fulfilling its sworn oath to "faithfully discharge the duties of the office." One of Congress' many duties is oversight of the executive branch of government. As our country was born upon the defeat of a monarch, the founders of the country considered Congressional oversight of the president to be an absolute given, and the Supreme Court has subsequently reaffirmed this duty. One must ask herself, "Why is Trump so skittish about further investigation? Once again, he *"doth protest too much."*

Furthermore, on May 22, 2019, recall that Trump walked out of a meeting with Congressional leaders about improving the country's infrastructure. This is an absolutely essential topic that must be addressed, yet Trump huffed out of the meeting before it could start. He was upset by a comment that Speaker Pelosi had made prior to the meeting which implied that she intended to investigate leads that Mueller documented. Trump walked to microphones outside of the meeting room and said that Congress essentially had two choices:

(a) legislation (if this choice was selected, Trump would actually do his job and Congress would have the "honor" of working with him to address the country's many problems); or

(b) investigation (if this choice was selected, Trump essentially said he would not be able to sit down to do the people's work with Congress).

In other words, Trump threatened that he would not uphold his presidential oath ("faithfully execute the Office of President" by working with Congress to solve problems) if Congress did uphold its oath ("faithfully discharge the duties of the office" by taking steps to oversee the executive branch). Outside of everything else, this purposeful failure to perform his duty as President should be enough for impeachment consideration alone.

My Ask:

Please read the Mueller Report. At least read the summaries of the two main sections. If you don't read it, please download the free audiobook version[43] of it and listen to it in the car.

I also ask that you not be one of the people who fall for the political spin associated with the Mueller Report. Recognize when you are being fed talking points. Again, please read the actual report and ask yourself if Trump's actions described in the report are truly worthy of the Office of the Presidency. I do not believe they should be.

If Trump is re-elected, you can all but guarantee that his endless controversies (including continued impeachment consideration) will not magically disappear. If ongoing controversy was your concern about Hillary Clinton in 2016, you must see that it is exponentially worse with Trump.

We as a country simply need to move on, right?

---

[43] https://www.amazon.com/Mueller-Report-Findings-Special-Investigation/dp/B07NMVF5SQ/ref=sr_1_3?crid=3SD6ZWC5CYZG0&keywords=mueller+report+audible&qid=1560186883&s=books&sprefix=muell%2Caudible%2C198&sr=1-3

12. "Trump will surround himself with smart people."

When I heard people say this about Trump before the election, I immediately recognized it for what it was. This hopeful pondering was an implicit admission that the Trump didn't know what the hell he would be doing as president – and that he needed smart people around him to guard the country against some of his more stupid impulses.

2019 Update:
OK, so who are these smart people that surround him? Whom does he allow to have influence on his thinking?

– Who Trump Listens To –

(1) The first answer is Donald J. Trump.

A March 13, 2016 *Politico* article[44] includes the following look into Trump's thinking:

"Asked on MSNBC's 'Morning Joe' who he talks with consistently about foreign policy, Trump responded, "I'm speaking with myself, number one, because I have a very good brain and I've said a lot of things."...

"I know what I'm doing and I listen to a lot of people, I talk to a lot of people and at the appropriate time I'll tell you who the people are," Trump said. "But my primary consultant is myself and I have a good instinct for this stuff."

---

[44] https://www.politico.com/blogs/2016-gop-primary-live-updates-and-results/2016/03/trump-foreign-policy-adviser-220853

Read what you want into that quote, but it seems clear to me that he has an exaggerated estimation of his own experience. If you have not seen it before, I recommend that you watch the referenced video from "*Vice News*"[45] which compiles some of the things Donald Trump claims he is the best in the world at doing (or knowing).

These include being the best at:
"(1) being strong,
(2) having good toys,
(3) the military,
(4) loving the Bible,
(5) building walls,
(6) helping the disabled,
(7) fighting for veterans,
(8) promoting equality,
(9) supporting Israel,
(10) being conservative,
(11) respecting women,
(12) being tough on ISIS,
(13) getting crowds,
(14) understanding nuclear horror,
(15) understanding devaluation,
(16) understanding uranium sales,
(17) understanding trade,
(18) understanding the game,
(19) understanding infrastructure,
(20) understanding visas,
(21) understanding politicians,
(22) understanding taxes,

[45] https://www.youtube.com/watch?v=YA631bMT9g8

(23) understanding debt, and
(24) understanding the system."

How anyone can read all this and still see Trump as anything other than a conman (and/or a crazy man) of historic proportions astounds me.

Well, maybe this all makes sense. After all, perhaps Trump's "very large brain" is simply too big to allow other brains to fit in the room. It is too bad though that he apparently can still fit a TV in the bedroom. It appears that the brains over at Fox News can still get through to him across the air waves.

(2) Trump is clearly influenced by Fox News personnel.

A quick search on the Trump Twitter Archive[46] website shows that he has (as of June 12, 2019) tweeted or re-tweeted @FoxNews 650 times, @foxandfriends 542 times, @seanhannity 192 times, @tuckercarlson 30 times, and @judgejeanine 27 times. Every one of these tweets that I read conveyed a positive tone regarding these Fox-related twitter handles. On the other hand, @nytimes is tweeted or retweeted 146 times, but of these, almost half of these (72 of the 146) have the word "Failing" immediately before the @nytimes twitter handle.

One example of Fox News' influence on Trump policy is noted below. On August 22, 2018, Trump tweeted the following:

---

[46] http://www.trumptwitterarchive.com/archive

"I have asked Secretary of State @SecPompeo to closely study the South Africa land and farm seizures and expropriations and the large scale killing of farmers. 'South African Government is now seizing land from white farmers.' @TuckerCarlson @FoxNews"

As fate would have it, it turns out that Tucker Carlson had just discussed this topic on his show earlier the very same day. Go figure!

Mere hours after Trump's tweet, the South African government tweeted the following response:

"South Africa totally rejects this narrow perception which only seeks to divide our nation and reminds us of our colonial past. #landexpropriation @realDonaldTrump @PresidencyZA"

Surprise surprise, it appears that Carlson's reporting was misleading at best. Fact-checking website Snopes found the claim that "A 'large-scale killing' of white farmers is taking place in South Africa" to be False[47]. Note that the Snopes truth grading system is more nuanced than a simple true or false option. Options include "True," "Mostly True," "Mixture," "Mostly False," "False," and 'Unproven." A rating of "False," therefore, really leaves no room for grey half-truths or any "well, it is complicated" nuanced explanations. It simply is just false.

[47] https://www.snopes.com/fact-check/white-farmers-south-africa/

- Only the best and smartest people? –

For a person who promised that he would only bring in the best and smartest people, let's look at what Trump's own words say about people that he himself chose to bring into his orbit on behalf of the American people.

(1) Rex Tillerson,
Secretary of State,
February 1, 2017 to March 13, 2018:

> *"Rex Tillerson, a man who is 'dumb as a rock' and totally ill prepared and ill equipped to be Secretary of State..."* (Twitter; May 23, 2019)

(2) Jeff Sessions,
Attorney General,
February 8, 2017 to November 7, 2018:

> *(a) "Sessions didn't have a clue!"*
> (Twitter; March 8, 2019)
>
> *(b) "... who was hired by Jeff Sessions (another beauty) ..."* (Twitter; February 18, 2019)
>
> *(c) "Jeff Sessions doesn't understand what is happening underneath his command position..."*
> (Twitter; August 25,2018)

(3) Steve Bannon,
White House Chief Strategist,
January 20, 2017 to August 18, 2017:

(a) "The Mercer Family recently dumped the leaker known as Sloppy Steve Bannon. Smart!" (Twitter; January 5, 2018)

(b) "Michael Wolff is a total loser who made up stories in order to sell this really boring and untruthful book. He used Sloppy Steve Bannon, who cried when he got fired and begged for his job. Now Sloppy Steve has been dumped like a dog by almost everyone. Too bad!" (Twitter; January 5, 2018)

Only the best and the brightest I see... and remember that this is all coming from Trump's own twitter-fingers. There are seemingly endless examples of Trump praising others and then demeaning them...or vice versa.

He attacked Ben Carson as unstable and crazy on Twitter (see Trump's November 6, 2015 tweet: *"With Ben Carson wanting to hit his mother on head with a hammer, stab a friend and Pyramids built for grain storage - don't people get it?"*) and then he hires him to run Housing and Urban Development (HUD).

Trump implies that former Texas Governor Rick Perry is a failure and an idiot. Then he hires him to be the Secretary of Energy.

Don't get me started on Trump's change of tune on his own personal lawyer, Michael Cohen. Cohen was his right-hand man for more than a decade, until he became a "rat." Even if you only used Trump's own words against him, Trump clearly has colossally terrible judgement.

There is an obvious pattern here for those willing to take their hands from their eyes, and it leads to an obvious conclusion. Trump doesn't care one bit about getting expert counsel for the betterment of the country. The "best and brightest" claim was for campaign bumper stickers and that's it.

He put lobbyist Scott Pruitt, a non-scientist who rejects the scientific consensus about climate change, in charge of the Environmental Protection Agency.

He put lobbyist Betsy DeVos, a woman who during her confirmation hearing showed that she was not even aware of one of the largest debates within the educational community ("growth-vs-proficiency"), as Secretary of Education.

And as mentioned earlier, he put Ben Carson, a man with no professional background at all in the housing industry, in charge of HUD.

Two traits in common with each of these listed above are: (1) they were wholly unqualified for the positions for which Trump nominated them, and (2) they financially and/or politically supported Trump for president.

Trump likes to compare himself to Abraham Lincoln, but whereas Lincoln was known to have specifically sought out qualified people to argue for perspectives other than his own, Trump does the exact opposite. Trump wants "yes-men" and "yes-women" only. Trump cares about propping up those people that he thinks will embellish the "Trump-is-great" narrative and once they no longer serve that purpose, they're gone.

After firing Jeff Sessions, Trump essentially admitted that he hired him as the Attorney General – not because he was qualified for the job – but because Trump thought he'd be getting a perpetual "yes-man" due to Session's perceived "loyalty":

> *"The only reason I gave him the job, because I felt loyalty. He was an original supporter. He was on the campaign."*[48]

You could easily have missed it if you weren't paying attention, but I think I remember that part of the rallying chant at Trump's campaign rallies.

> *"Drain the Swamp! Drain the Swamp! Drain the Swamp (unless your guy was loyal to you... then you can sneak him in... we won't tell), Drain the Swamp! Drain the Swamp! ..."*

– More on the swamp –

How many times during the campaign did Trump claim that he would be "draining the swamp" of lobbyists and "the Washington establishment"? A lot! He was super rich after all (i.e. "*The beauty of me is that I am very rich*"[49]) so he would not be influenced, he claimed, by lobbyists with money. So has Trump been the "roto-rooter" extraordinaire? Is the swamp drain working?

No... and no.

---

[48] https://www.businessinsider.com/trump-sessions-hired-him-because-loyalty-supporter-2018-8

[49] https://www.youtube.com/watch?v=wjWfSZT1obA

Turns out that Trump once again has "talked it" but has not "walked it." Despite his big talk about an ethics proposal that may have sounded good, only a small portion of it has been implemented, and there appears to be no sense of urgency to further address the issue. In fact, lobbyists seem to be thriving. An October 19, 2017 Politico article [50] quotes Republican lobbyist Brian Wild as saying,

"I don't think that anything's really changed... If anything, the lobbying business is booming right now."

Since Trump has taken office, he has actually made it easier to waive the required lobbyist waiting period[51] (this is the period between 'being in office' and 'being a paid lobbyist'). Under Obama, waivers could be made but there needed to be transparent documentation explaining the reasons for the waiver. Under Trump, this level of transparency is no longer required.

A January 30, 2019 marketwatch.com article[52] summarizes the "revolving door" of lobbyists for each presidential administration going back approximately 45 years to President Ford. The author defines this "revolving door" as "*the number of individuals in each administration who worked in the influence industry before or after their government jobs.*"

The results are not favorable to Trump. These revolving door individuals total 326 over Trump's first 2-years in office

---

[50] https://www.politico.com/story/2017/10/19/trump-drain-swamp-promises-243924

[51] https://www.politico.com/story/2017/01/trump-lobbying-ban-weakens-obama-ethics-rules-234318

[52] https://www.marketwatch.com/story/how-the-trump-presidency-ranks-against-prior-administrations-in-links-to-lobbyists-in-one-chart-2019-01-18

– a pace of 163 individuals per year. That is almost three times more than the average of the seven prior administrations in the analysis and almost 30% more than experienced under George W. Bush (the administration with the next highest rate).

Lobbyists are not bad people by definition, and many of them may be doing good with their work. As someone who campaigned about draining the swamp of government-types such as career lobbyists, however, this is a very clear black eye for Trump.

- Exceedingly high staff turnover –

I believe the above establishes that: Trump does NOT appear to seek counsel from experts, Trump is NOT surrounding himself with the best and brightest, and Trump is flooding the swamp. Another factor to consider though is that many of the people that Trump does surround himself with, don't tend to stay with him for very long. Case in point, as I write this today on June 13, 2019, the breaking news is that the White House Press Secretary, Sarah Sanders, has just resigned.

The Brookings Institute published a study tracking the staff turnover in the most recent presidential administrations from Reagan to Trump. The study[53] breaks staff into two main categories: (a) senior-level positions that are not cabinet positions and (b) cabinet positions.

---

[53] https://www.brookings.edu/research/tracking-turnover-in-the-trump-administration/

An analysis of their findings shows that the turnover rate of senior level positions for the first two years of a presidential administration is 83% higher (almost double) under Trump than under the average of the previous presidents dating back to Reagan. The story is even worse for cabinet-level positions. The turnover rate under Trump is five times higher than under the average presidency in the study.

The data shows that of the people that leave Trump's administration for which their conditions of departure are known, almost twice as many resigned than were fired[54]. Either way, Trump likes to try to spin things so to say that such a ridiculous turnover rate somehow helps the efficiency of his administration. Anyone who has ever attempted to work as part of a team with ongoing turnover at the top knows this is inherently untrue.

– Exceedingly slow nomination and position fulfillment –

Vacancies. Help Needed. Now I believe we have established that: Trump does NOT appear to seek counsel from experts, Trump is NOT surrounding himself with the best and brightest, Trump is flooding the swamp, and Trump has a staff turnover rate that is unprecedented in recent presidential history. Let's add one more to that list.

The Trump administration has been historically slow (among recent presidents) in both (a) nominating people for positions and (b) in actually getting these positions filled. The White House Transition Project[55] compared job vacancy

[54] https://www.cnn.com/interactive/2017/08/politics/trump-admin-departures-trnd/

rates for Presidents Reagan through Trump. An analysis of the presented data shows that Trump is 20% slower than the average of these presidential administrations on the nomination process and 40% slower than the average with regards to closing the deal and filling positions. Trump, who also likes to compare himself with Reagan, is at approximately half of the position fill-rate that Reagan was after two years.

There have been a number of people who have reportedly turned down job offers from President Trump. I suspect that some people – including conservative-leaning individuals – do not want to be associated with the Trump administration and this may be a real factor in the number of current job vacancies.

– Summary –

Trump does NOT appear to seek counsel from experts, Trump is NOT surrounding himself with the best and brightest, Trump is flooding the swamp, Trump has a staff turnover rate that is unprecedented in recent presidential history, and Trump has been historically slow in both nominating for job vacancies and in closing the deal to fill them.

The idea that the Trump administration is a well-oiled machine as he claims can only be true if that machine is a century-old, barely operating merry-go-round with an oil intake that has been long rusted through with holes. Trump

---

[55] http://www.whitehousetransitionproject.org/appointments/

isolates himself from people that could advise him... and more and more, he is isolating himself from reality as well.

If this "surrounded-by-smart-people" argument was one of the reasons you allowed yourself to vote for Trump in 2016, please now ask yourself the following question.

Did the hope you had that he'd surround himself with smart people mask the fear you had that he would act on his worst impulses?

It was often argued at the time that it would be OK because there would be "adults in the room." Trump has shown now that he is even worse than the toddler some of us feared. He is a toddler with a gun, and he has been shooting the adults in the room since taking office.

My Ask:

Please understand that there is no hint whatsoever that Trump will change if re-elected in 2020. He will not have a change of heart, suddenly become another person, and take important input from experts. He is propped up by a house of cards, with more and more cards dropping by the day. He is truly an existential threat to our system of government.

I suspect that some of you will think such a statement is going too far. It is not. By doing things such as attempting to block people from properly responding to Congressional subpoenas, Trump is, right now, challenging the very nature of the checks and balances designed by our Constitution.

Having said this, I want to specifically address a portion of my intended audience that might be A-OK with blowing up the current system of government. A portion of Trump voters have a libertarian streak and believe that "government is the problem." For these folks, I ask that you please understand what you are saying here. Our system of government, imperfect as it may be, has created one of the longest-lasting, generally-free societies in history. If you truly love freedom as you likely proclaim, you'd do well to remember that.

Trump checks many of the boxes of dictatorship (such as demonization of the free press). When governments fall, they don't typically fall easily. In your zest for more freedom, you may end up with a despot who takes your freedom. Also, recognize Trump's part in damaging our system of government and that damaged prey wet the lips of waiting predators. Putin I'm sure is salivating. I ask that you watch what you wish for.

13. "Trump is a patriot."

Some people believed that Trump was a patriot because he talked about "America first" and hugged flags at his rallies.

2019 Update:
Trump is no patriot. I should be able to stop there. By now, I'd hope this would be clear. Trump is no patriot. He is a "Trumpiot" and that's it.

Trump lies to the American people multiple times a day. He kowtows to foreign dictators and adversaries and he trusts them over American intelligence agencies. Just yesterday (June 12, 2019), he said there would be nothing wrong accepting assistance from Russia (again) with regards to upcoming elections, and he would not say that he'd tell the FBI if this were to occur (again).

Trump says this even though U.S. intelligence is crystal clear that Russia committed crimes while purposefully and successfully seeking to influence the American voters against Clinton and for Trump in 2016 by spreading false information (and also stolen information). Keep in mind as well that Trump says this only days after a Russian destroyer and a U.S. missile cruiser nearly crashed after an aggressive maneuver by the Russian ship (on June 7, 2019).

Trump pumps his chest and imagines himself a big tough military guy, yet he evaded the Vietnam War and he criticizes fallen military heroes and their families frequently.

He also promised to look out for veterans using V.A. services, but he broke this promise by allowing hundreds of thousands of records to be purged, extending the bureaucratic nightmare for these veterans.

He is destabilizing relationships with close allies that the United States has had for decades, if not centuries. He scoffs at the separation of powers specifically designed by the country's founders. He seeks to arm a foreign regime (Saudi Arabia) with nuclear weapons technology while that regime has been found responsible by U.S. intelligence for the calculated murder of a journalist living in the United States. He also wants to limit free speech, especially when that speech is critical of him.

My Ask:

Please don't let stupid things (like Trump redesigning Air Force One with more red-white-and-blue paint) lull you into thinking Trump is a patriot. This is a man that breaks his oath of office on a regular basis. If this man is a patriot, he is a Russian one.

14. “The Supreme Court”

Leading up to the 2016 election, a friend expressed that he did not like Trump, but he felt that Trump would nominate conservative judges to the Supreme Court of the United States (SCOTUS), and he was therefore considering voting for him with the “political long game” in mind. My friend was not alone in this thinking. Many Trump voters held their noses and looked away while voting, but they nonetheless left the booth having pulled the lever for Trump.

2019 Update:

I must admit that this one is a bit different than the others. Whereas Trump has clearly demonstrated that he did not live up to many of the expectations noted in this book, he did come through in this case. If you voted for Trump because you thought he’d nominate conservative-leaning judges, you were correct. Trump nominated Judges Neil Gorsuch and Brett Kavanaugh and was able to get them both confirmed through the Senate.

– Goal achieved –

(1) Although the Supreme Court is specifically supposed to be non-partisan, presidents will rarely nominate someone who does not share their general take on how the Constitution should be interpreted. I hesitate to do it because of the goal of nonpartisanship, but for ease of reference I will refer to Supreme Court judges that were nominated by Republican administrations as “R-judges” and those that were nominated by Democratic administrations as “D-judges.” Currently, we have five R-judges and four D-

judges. This said, the goal of a "conservative-leaning" SCOTUS has already been achieved.

(2) Because the appointment can be a life-time appointment if the judge is not impeached or does not retire, the age and health of the judges do factor into the calculus. Currently, the average age of the R-judges is ten years younger than the average age of the D-judges. In fact, the oldest R-judge, Judge Clarence Thomas, is younger than the average age of all the D-judges. This said, there will likely be conservative-leaning judges in SCOTUS for some time.

(3) The Senate is the branch of Congress responsible for confirming Supreme Court nominees. All that is needed for confirmation is 51 of the 100 Senate votes. Currently, Republicans hold the majority, and this is not expected to change in 2020 given the senate seats that are up for election. This means that even if a left-leaning president wins in 2020 and a SCOTUS seat becomes vacant, it would be difficult for the new president to get a "D-judge" confirmed with a Republican-majority senate. If you don't believe me, ask Merrick Garland [56].

Given the above, I'd say that this specific reason for voting Trump in 2016 has already been achieved and it is therefore not a valid reason to vote for Trump in 2020.

- For those who want more –

I suspect some of you are not on board with my conclusion. I can see the "wait a minute... not so fast"

[56] https://en.wikipedia.org/wiki/Merrick_Garland

thought-bubbles above some of you reading this. Some of you would say the SCOTUS needs to be loaded with conservative judges and a simple majority is not enough... that we need a massively conservative-leaning SCOTUS.

Before I address this, I feel I must first address those among you who may be so-called “one-issue” voters. The so-called “one-issue” might be the economy, the military, or any other issue. In my experience, however, the “one-issue” is usually “abortion rights” (and sometimes, “gun rights”). The thought is that SCOTUS may make decisions that could impact this one issue you care about, so regardless of nearly everything else going on in the country and world, you may vote in hopes to lean the scales towards a SCOTUS that is more in line with your take on that one issue.

<u>I acknowledge that this section below does indeed veer quite a bit from Trump specifically as a topic, but I find this discussion necessary as it is the “elephant in the room” for many people that voted for Trump in 2016.</u>

<u>I. Abortion:</u>

For some, this is the most taboo topic in American politics. I do not expect that anything I write below will make you do a 180-degree shift from your current stance on the issue. If you voted for Trump because of this issue, you likely are firmly in the pro-life camp. Nonetheless, I think it is worthwhile to make the following points.

(1) I use the terms “pro-life” and “pro-choice” in this section for ease of reference only. Those terms are clearly

handcuffed by their connotations. The pro-choice side will argue that they are pro-life (for the mother). The pro-life side will argue that women do have a choice to not be a mother by not having sex (unless they are raped, that is).

(2) Many people argue for the overturning of *Roe vs Wade* without knowing that the case only fully protects abortion rights in the first trimester (0-12 weeks). Federal protections generally decrease as the pregnancy continues. Rights to an abortion in the second trimester (13-25 weeks), for example, are generally protected, but now certain state restrictions are permitted. In the third trimester (26-40 weeks), states can actually disallow abortions, as long as certain protections for the health of the mother are made.

(3) In 2018, Ireland, a predominately Catholic country, voted to make abortion at least partially legal, so it is understandable that the topic frequently made the news that year. In a May 24, 2018 *Irish Times* article[57], Dr Tomás Ryan of Trinity College Dublin cut to some of the details:

> *"Crucially, the coordinated brain activity required for consciousness does not occur until 24-25 weeks of pregnancy. We cannot say when consciousness first emerges, but it cannot rationally be called before the end of the second trimester at 24 weeks of pregnancy."*

(4) Given the points above, *Roe vs Wade* only federally protects a women's ability to have a legal abortion during

---

[57] https://www.irishtimes.com/opinion/the-moment-a-baby-s-brain-starts-to-function-and-other-scientific-answers-on-abortion-1.3506968

the time when it is likely scientifically impossible for the fetus to have consciousness.

(5) The Centers for Disease Control and Prevention (CDC) reported 2015 data[58] that showed that almost two-thirds of abortions occurred less than eight weeks into the "gestation period" and only 1.3% of the cases occur after 21 weeks.

(6) Of those very rare cases that do occur after 21 weeks, they frequently happen when (a) the mother's health is in danger and/or (b) the fetus has such physical defects that it/she/he would not be expected to survive long after birth. Perhaps no lungs are present, or the fetus' internal organs develop separately outside of the body.

(7) I used to be Catholic, and in this last case of fetuses that are not viable due to severe physical defects, I see significant parallels with Catholic teaching on end-of-life decisions. If you read paragraphs 2278 and 2279 of the "Catechism of the Catholic Church: Second Edition"[59], you will see that the Church essentially accepts the following:

(a) "*alleviating suffering of the dying, even at the risk of shortening their days,*" and
(b) "*discontinuing medical procedures that are burdensome, dangerous, extraordinary, or disproportionate to the expected outcome.*"

I recall learning in Catholic school that these teachings meant it was acceptable by the Church to take someone off

---

[58] https://www.cdc.gov/mmwr/volumes/67/ss/ss6713a1.htm#T7_down
[59] http://www.scborromeo.org/ccc/p3s2c2a5.htm

of life-support machines to allow the inevitable death to occur. In the case of a fetus, the woman's body IS the life-support system (via the umbilical cord). Removing the fetus from life-support in these situations (cutting the cord) to end future suffering seems in-line with these Catholic teachings.

The potential psychological suffering of the mother (and even the father as well) should also be considered. The mother, after all, is not just a life-support machine but is her own person herself. This fact often seems to be quickly glossed over by many in the pro-life movement. Parents being forced to watch their child be born, suffer, and then die, when much of that suffering could have been prevented, seems cruel all around.

(8) Lastly, if you are someone who believes that a human soul is present at the moment of conception, I understand that it would be hard for you to vote for someone who seems callously unconcerned about what you consider to be the murder of human beings. With the demonization of each side by the other, I believe it may be difficult for some pro-choice people to understand that you as a pro-lifer (if you are one) truly believe you are voting to save human lives. I went with other students from my Catholic college to the annual 'March for Life' in Washington, DC when I was younger, and I remember having those same thoughts myself. I could not understand how other people could see it any other way.

To these folks I offer the following summary of a thought-experiment you may have seen by author, Patrick Tomlinson, on Twitter in 2017:

You are in a fertility clinic that is on fire. On your way running out you open a door and see a young child in one corner and box with a note that reads "1000 viable human embryos." The fire is getting close and you only have time to either get the child or the box. Is it more morally acceptable to save the child or the box?

The implied – and I believe "correct" moral answer – is to save the child. The intent of the thought experiment is to show that when truly forced to think about it, we do not hold a "human life" embryo as having equal worth as a "human life" child. This then undercuts the argument that all "human life" (even in its embryonic stage) is to be equally protected under the law.

I have read articles attempting to contest the logic of this thought experiment, but I find these counter arguments quite weak. I reference links[60] to some [61] of these articles herein, but I will not go into a rebuttal against them here as I have already strayed pretty far from Trump and I want to move on to other topics.

---

[60] https://thefederalist.com/2017/10/18/no-saving-child-instead-embryos-burning-building-not-negate-pro-life-position/

[61] https://www.weeklystandard.com/berny-belvedere/heres-an-honest-answer-to-that-dumb-twitter-rant-on-abortion

II. Gun Rights:

In my mind, "gun rights" run a far second to "abortion" as being the one-issue voter's one issue. That said, I've had multiple debates with folks about the second amendment (usually after a terrible gun tragedy such as the La Vegas shooting on October 1, 2017), and I have come to see just how fevered certain people get when the topic of gun restrictions comes up.

Several of these debates have taken place on social media with people that I do not personally know well, but it is still clear just how drastically different we view guns. I recognize, for example, that I might be more defensive about people wanting to restrict access to my weapons if I was a soldier.

When I think of my weapons, I think of them as being dangerous and potentially falling into the wrong hands. A soldier, however, might see her gun as a tool that allowed her to save someone's life – or her own life – in war. The perceived connotations associated with guns in these two cases are drastically different. People are certainly coming from different starting points on this issue.

All that said, there generally is bipartisan support for certain gun control regulations among the American people. Some "common sense" gun control ideas that have significant support among Americans include closing loopholes that allow:

(1) people with mental illness to own firearms,
(2) people who are on a no-fly list to own firearms, and
(3) people who could not purchase a certain weapon over the counter to buy said weapon from a friend or at a gun show.

Unfortunately, the National Rifle Association (NRA) does not concur with some of these ideas. Because they fund many a political campaign, the elected officials they support may be reluctant to take up the cause while in office.

Now that the Supreme Court has more "R-judges" than "D-judges," it does appear that "pro-gun" activists will attempt to challenge certain state laws in the Supreme Court. The "New York State Rifle & Pistol Association," for example, is doing this very thing in New York right now. That said, I do not think most Trump-friendly voters typically view the gun control issue on par with the abortion issue... but I could be wrong. I think some Trump supporters could prop up almost any issue as THE one-issue if they thought it would get Trump re-elected.

Abortion (in most cases) is legally protected in the U.S. and pro-life activists are aiming to take away that legal right. *District of Columbia vs Heller,* which is perhaps the closest thing to a gun right's version of *Roe vs Wade*, is already on the books as reaffirming gun ownership rights. The legal burden, therefore, is on those on the left to challenge in the courts. Successfully doing so is unlikely given the current make-up of the conservative-leaning SCOTUS.

Given the significant consensus among Americans on many of the key gun control issues (such as those discussed in this chapter), it is most likely that many of the hot buttons will eventually hash out in Congress (not SCOTUS) anyway. I say this, while still acknowledging that the political power of the NRA is still significant, despite recent reports that it is losing its financial footing.

- Trump, checks, and balances –

If you voted for Trump because you liked the chances that he could have an influence on the make-up of the Supreme Court, I suspect that you inherently recognized the importance of the Supreme Court as a check against the other two branches of government. The checks and balances of our three-branch system is perhaps the crowning jewel of our country's government. Donald Trump apparently does not share this appreciation for the three-branch system, despite his oath to protect the Constitution which set up this system in the first place.

Trump encourages (and/or directs) staff to defy Congressional subpoenas and he refuses to work with Congress on important issues while Congress is attempting to provide a check against his power. His attack on Congress is clear, but he is also on record slandering the judicial branch as well.

He has been open in his criticism of Chief Justice Roberts, and his general maligning of the judicial branch and/or individual judges (i.e. Judge Gonzalo Curiel) is well documented. It should be noted that it is rare for a president to vocalize much of any opinion on the judicial branch at all, other than to say that he is appreciative that it stands as an independent branch of government. With the exception of nominating candidates to fill SCOTUS vacancies who align with their own perspectives, presidents have (at least publicly) respected the court as an apolitical and independent branch.

But Trump is different. Trump clearly sees the judicial branch as a political arm of government, but worse than this, he seems to see it as HIS political arm of government, one that he can swing as a weapon against his political rivals. I don't know if Judge Gorsuch or Judge Kavanaugh feel indebted to Trump for their current position, but it seems likely that Trump believes they should be. Trump takes credit for nearly everything and there is no shortage of evidence that he "expects loyalty" from those for whom he does "favors."

On April 24, 2019, Trump tweeted (with regard to the findings in the Mueller Report) that:

> *"If the partisan Dems ever tried to Impeach, I would first head to the U.S. Supreme Court."*

What he means by that is unclear. The right of Congress to impeach (and even remove) a president is crystal clear in the Constitution. It is difficult to imagine what case Trump would argue to SCOTUS if impeachment did become a reality. On one hand, Trump has spent much of his professional life threatening lawsuits, so it is not completely a surprise to see him do that here. On the other hand, though, this is quite concerning to see him doing this at this level.

I'd still see it as highly unlikely, but perhaps Trump could get a vote or two from SCOTUS in such a case due to Trump-nominated judges potentially feeling a need to "repay a debt" to him (regardless of the fact that there would be no real legal standing whatsoever to do so). In Trump's dream, he'd be able to stir up political tribalism enough to potentially impact all of SCOTUS in this way, and he would get the whole conservative majority to side with him (again, despite there being no real legal standing).

This chain of thought may seem really "out there" to some reading this and I do agree that it is unlikely, but it is not impossible. This clearly seems to be something that Trump would attempt to do under the circumstances. A president's undue influence over the courts is a clear road marker towards becoming a sham of a representative government. There is no magic that automatically prevents something like this from happening here... and then it would be goodbye to the U.S.A. as we know it.

Again, I see the above as very unlikely. I want to stress that once more, lest I be called an alarmist. That said, it is indeed alarming to witness a U.S. president that continually pushes to weaken the power of those governmental branches that were specifically designed to provide a check against his own power. This IS dangerous and destabilizing. Allowing Trump to get away with this behavior not only threatens the effectiveness of our division of power while Trump is president, it gives a roadmap to a future president

– possibly not of your political leanings – to do the same. Voting Trump for a second term in 2020 is tacit approval for this to occur.

My Ask:

You have a conservative-leaning court and SCOTUS will likely have a heavy conservative influence for years to come. With that being the case, I ask that you shift your view now to protecting SCOTUS as an institution (and Congress as well) from attack by the executive branch.

If you are a one-issue voter and you did not find my text regarding common one-issue-voter topics to be convincing, I ask that you at least consider no longer just focusing on a single issue when you vote. After all, what good in the long run does it do if you "save a fetus" one day, only to have that mother and fetus killed in a nuclear explosion the next day because our president couldn't control a temper tantrum? Remember this guy has the nuclear codes and the "adults in the room" are backed in the corner and/or perpetually have one foot out the door.

I also ask that you weigh all the incriminating information about the Mueller Report regarding Trump's own actions. If you can't bring yourself to vote for a Democrat, I ask that you write in a Republican or some other person who you do feel would be an effective and good leader.

Lastly, I ask that you do not simply dismiss as crazy certain proposals from the left regarding changes to SCOTUS. Putting 20-year term limits on a chief justice or adding more justices both could have an impact on lessening the power of each individual judge, while likely safeguarding the independence of the institution itself. If each judge has less power, her potential corruption as a judge would be of less import.

15. "Trump cares about me."

Many people felt that Trump really cared for them because he came to visit them in Wisconsin (or another lowly-populated state where they lived). I certainly agree that Trump acknowledged the pain of a certain group of people that did not feel like their voices were being heard. This no doubt had an enormous impact on him winning the election.

Trump was able to convince us that he was just like us. He convinced some military folks that a draft-dodger and mocker of military heroes was "for them." He convinced many poorer Americans that he was no "elitist" despite his silver spoon and his demonstrable history of not caring for the "little guy." Trump convinced many of us that he was a generous and charitable giver, yet theweek.com[62]reports that "*many charities that Trump claimed to have donated millions of dollars to said they never received the money.*" He also used charity funds (and a fake bidder) to bid up and then purchase a huge painting of himself.

But many people did not want to see this in 2016. Instead they saw themselves in Trump and they were hooked. The thinking went something like this:

He ate Kentucky Fried Chicken (KFC) just like us. He engaged in "locker room banter" about grabbing pussy like some of us (not me, for the record). *To hell with political*

[62] https://theweek.com/speedreads/813387/6-notsocharitable-things-trumps-charity-spent-money

correctness. He spoke directly to us. He was blunt and refreshing. He was just one of the guys.

2019 Update:

Read almost anything written in this book, and I hope that you can see by now that Trump cares about Trump alone, period... end of sentence. His self-centered nature is staggering. Case in point, he complains that Twitter is somehow against him because Obama has more followers than he does. This is absolutely infantile, and the jealousy can't help but be reminiscent of Nixon's apparent jealousy of Kennedy.

Simply put, Trump is perhaps the most effective conman in recent history. He is a narcissist who wants the world to revolve around him, and we have now put him in the position where it partially does. He throws tantrums about anything he doesn't like and skirts responsibilities for almost everything for which he is to blame.

My Ask:

If you find yourself thinking "well, all politicians are elitists or liars," please recognize that there is no chance of equivalency when compared to Trump.

Perhaps you recognize that Trump doesn't really care about you after all, but this is OK because you think you economically benefit from his policies. I ask that you re-read the section entitled "Trump will be good for the economy" and reconsider.

Conclusion

I will keep this conclusion short. I have essentially written this text in a two-week period in early June 2019 during nights, after work. It has been one of the freest flowing things I've written, and I think this is because so much of it has long been just under the surface for me. I, like many Americans, have had Trump occupy a portion of my thoughts since his campaign seemed viable. I could see the slow-moving train wreck coming, but it was too hard to process what I was seeing. Now, walking the wreckage, the surreal feeling has not left.

As I mentioned in the introduction, I specifically avoided some key issues in this book because I thought a portion of my target audience might lose interest if I had focused on them. The dog whistles to white nationalism are real and the examples of misogyny are too many to list, but I avoided these on purpose – also because much has already been written about them elsewhere.

There are other reasons of course that people voted for Trump not included in my list of fifteen. People believed, for example, that he would be tougher on terrorism, yet he has cozied up with a Saudi regime that has likely supported it[63]. Trump's very cult of personality also seems to have been an influence on certain acts of domestic terrorism[64] since he took office.

Lastly, I want to leave you with Trump's attack on the truth. Trump aimed to devalue truth and he has succeeded.

---

[63] https://www.nytimes.com/interactive/projects/documents/evidence-of-financial-links-between-saudi-royal-family-and-al-qaeda

[64] https://www.cnn.com/2018/10/26/politics/cesar-sayoc-white-van-stickers/index.html

News reporting that is based on clear evidence – even on words coming straight out of Trump's mouth – is "fake news." Extensive evidence that Trump has a disturbing and possibly compromised relationship with Russia exists, yet he claims that this also is "fake news." An objective review of climate data requires leaders to acknowledge the overwhelming scientific consensus that the changing global climate truly poses an existential threat to humanity, yet this is also just "fake news" or just more "crazy talk by the radical leftist commies."

Despite the common idea that us lowly people could never know the truth on an issue because... you know... "deep state" ... TRUTH DOES EXIST. I ask that you think critically, that you doggedly seek the truth, and that you recognize the importance of this upcoming election.

People like to say how things will always eventually work out for good, but I see no evidence to support that. Things "working out" does not magically happen. It requires self-honesty, hard work, debate, real engagement as citizens, and of course... your vote.

References

4. "Trump is an excellent businessman."

https://www.nytimes.com/interactive/2019/05/07/us/politics/donald-trump-taxes.html

https://www.nytimes.com/2019/05/08/us/politics/trump-tax-investigation.html

https://www.cnbc.com/2019/03/05/trump-rises-51-spots-on-forbes-billionaires-list-but-his-net-worth-stays-flat-at-3point1b.html

https://www.thebalance.com/stock-market-returns-by-year-2388543

https://millersamuel.com/wp-content/uploads/2012/01/Miller100yearsNYre.jpg

https://www.washingtonpost.com/politics/2016/live-updates/general-election/real-time-fact-checking-and-analysis-of-the-first-presidential-debate/fact-check-has-trump-declared-bankruptcy-four-or-six-times/?utm_term=.050fe7719036

6. "Trump will defend us & be tough on our adversaries."

https://www.politifact.com/truth-o-meter/article/2017/jul/06/17-intelligence-organizations-or-four-either-way-r/

https://www.vanityfair.com/news/2018/12/trump-hotel-saudi-arabia

https://www.politifact.com/truth-o-meter/statements/2018/oct/18/donald-trump/donald-trumps-claim-no-financial-interests-saudi-a/

https://www.cnn.com/2018/11/20/politics/trump-saudi-arabia/index.html

https://www.cnn.com/2018/11/20/politics/trump-statement-saudi-khashoggi/index.html

https://www.washingtonpost.com/world/national-security/trump-approved-sharing-sensitive-nuclear-technology-with-saudi-arabia-after-khashoggi-murder/2019/06/04/d7b76676-86ef-11e9-a870-b9c411dc4312_story.html?utm_term=.97d90221c1c5

https://abcnews.go.com/Politics/trump-administration-approved-nuclear-deals-saudi-arabia-khashoggi/story?id=63492793

https://www.cnn.com/2019/04/26/middleeast/saudi-executions-court-documents-intl/index.html

https://en.wikipedia.org/wiki/Death_penalty_for_homosexuality

https://www.newsweek.com/philippine-president-duterte-tells-soldiers-wounded-fighting-islamist-extremists-im-here-die-1442263

7. "Trump will support the military."

https://www.cnn.com/interactive/2017/08/politics/trump-admin-departures-trnd/

https://fox2now.com/2019/03/05/president-pressured-staff-to-grant-security-clearance-to-ivanka-trump/

https://www.politico.com/story/2019/04/29/mueller-report-jared-kushner-dmitri-simes-russia-1291392

https://www.npr.org/2019/03/01/699407475/what-you-need-to-know-about-security-clearances-inside-and-outside-the-white-hou

https://www.apnews.com/1759ac2858ee4aafb041f91cbd6d86e9

https://www.cnn.com/interactive/2017/08/politics/trump-admin-departures-trnd/

https://www.washingtonexaminer.com/opinion/op-eds/trump-administration-breaks-campaign-promise-purges-200-000-va-healthcare-applications

https://www.nytimes.com/2016/08/02/us/politics/donald-trump-draft-record.html

https://www.nytimes.com/2018/12/26/us/politics/trump-vietnam-draft-exemption.html

https://www.businessinsider.com/putin-trump-polar-reactions-north-korean-general-salute-2019-4

https://www.nytimes.com/2018/11/16/us/politics/president-trump-military.html

https://www.cnn.com/2019/04/26/politics/military-families-tax-change-trump/index.html

https://thehill.com/homenews/administration/447025-trump-says-he-wouldve-been-honored-to-serve-in-military-thinks-hes

https://www.politifact.com/truth-o-meter/article/2018/nov/26/closer-look-donald-trumps-record-military-veterans/

https://www.politifact.com/truth-o-meter/statements/2018/may/10/donald-trump/did-donald-trump-sign-first-military-pay-raise-10-/

https://www.theguardian.com/commentisfree/2019/mar/27/trump-budget-military-immoral

https://www.mentalhealth.va.gov/suicide_prevention/data.asp

https://en.wikipedia.org/wiki/United_States_military_veteran_suicide

https://www.ssa.gov/oact/cola/colaseries.html

https://www.militarytimes.com/pay-benefits/military-pay-center/2019/01/03/the-new-pay-raise-is-in-effect-heres-the-2019-basic-pay-chart/

http://time.com/5489492/trump-military-raise/

https://taxfoundation.org/look-ahead-expiring-tax-provisions/

https://www.militarytimes.com/pay-benefits/2019/02/04/military-tax-tips-new-tax-law-is-mostly-good-news/

8. "Trump will be good for the economy."

https://www.nytimes.com/2017/01/17/upshot/presidents-have-less-power-over-the-economy-than-you-might-think.html

https://www.thebalance.com/us-gdp-by-year-3305543

https://www.cnn.com/2019/03/12/politics/trump-economic-boom-obama-compare/index.html

https://www.investopedia.com/ask/answers/101314/where-was-dow-jones-when-obama-took-office.asp

https://www.cnbc.com/2019/03/29/corporate-americas-best-tax-days-may-be-over-when-gop-tax-cuts-expire.html

https://www.economist.com/content/global_debt_clock

https://www.thebalance.com/trump-plans-to-reduce-national-debt-4114401

https://www.crfb.org/blogs/trump-will-face-highest-debt-gdp-ratio-any-new-president-truman

https://www.thebalance.com/trump-s-tax-plan-how-it-affects-you-4113968

http://fortune.com/2017/03/29/president-trump-job-claims-fact-check/

https://www.bloomberg.com/features/trump-tweets-market/

https://www.thestreet.com/investing/longest-bull-market-14804308

http://www.trumptwitterarchive.com/

https://taxfoundation.org/look-ahead-expiring-tax-provisions/

https://www.thebalance.com/national-debt-by-year-compared-to-gdp-and-major-events-3306287

https://www.cnbc.com/2019/06/07/trump-plays-risky-game-by-weaponizing-tariffs.html

https://www.thedrive.com/news/27003/trump-wants-nothing-to-do-with-crazy-driverless-cars-report

9. "I'm sticking with the home team (Republicans)."

https://www.cnn.com/videos/media/2019/06/09/laura-ingraham-trump-d-day-fox-news-interview-fake-news-sot-rs-vpx.cnn

https://theweek.com/articles/785361/how-trump-changing-republican-party-values

https://www.azcentral.com/story/news/politics/arizona/2018/05/12/ailing-sen-john-mccain-makes-final-plea-immigration-reform/583957002/

11. "A Clinton presidency would be mired in controversy."

https://www.pbs.org/newshour/politics/how-michael-cohen-broke-campaign-finance-law

https://www.nbcnews.com/think/opinion/mueller-report-proves-trump-failed-sound-alarm-russia-impeachable-offense-ncna997076

https://slate.com/news-and-politics/2019/04/mueller-report-paul-manafort.html

https://www.apnews.com/e0d125d737be4a21a81bec3d9f1dffd8

https://www.npr.org/sections/thetwo-way/2017/10/16/558228064/callista-gingrich-confirmed-as-ambassador-to-the-vatican

https://www.foxnews.com/opinion/newt-gingrich-mueller-tries-desperately-to-continue-bogus-russia-collusion-narrative-against-trump

https://thehill.com/homenews/media/382809-gingrich-compares-fbi-raid-of-trump-lawyer-to-nazi-secret-police

https://www.huffpost.com/entry/newt-gingrich-president-trump-twitter_n_5cef0ef1e4b00cfa1965bf9b

https://www.nbcnews.com/politics/politics-news/what-mueller-report-says-about-jared-kushner-ivanka-trump-donald-n995866

https://www.cnn.com/2019/06/04/politics/hope-hicks-annie-donaldson-white-house-documents/index.html

https://www.biography.com/news/salem-witch-trials-facts

https://www.facebook.com/watch/?v=740828706283857

https://www.cnbc.com/2019/05/22/trump-hosts-democratic-leaders-at-white-house-infrastructure-talks.html

12. "Trump will surround himself with smart people."

https://www.politico.com/blogs/2016-gop-primary-live-updates-and-results/2016/03/trump-foreign-policy-adviser-220853

https://www.abc.net.au/news/2019-06-13/trump-wants-pompeo-to-study-killing-of-farmers/10158114

https://www.news24.com/Analysis/expropriation-without-compensation-fact-checking-tucker-carlson-and-donald-trump-20180823

https://www.politico.com/story/2017/01/trump-lobbying-ban-weakens-obama-ethics-rules-234318

https://thinkprogress.org/trump-says-he-only-picked-sessions-to-be-ag-because-he-thought-he-would-be-loyal-987d897b81a0/

https://en.m.wikipedia.org/wiki/Administrator_of_the_Environmental_Protection_Agency

https://www.politico.com/story/2016/12/trump-tillerson-ethics-stocks-232595

https://www.cnn.com/2019/01/11/politics/temps-and-vacancies/index.html

https://www.newsweek.com/donald-trump-blows-ronald-reagan-away-conservatives-credit-1234137

14. "The Supreme Court"

https://thefederalist.com/2017/10/18/no-saving-child-instead-embryos-burning-building-not-negate-pro-life-position/

https://www.weeklystandard.com/berny-belvedere/heres-an-honest-answer-to-that-dumb-twitter-rant-on-abortion

https://www.guttmacher.org/fact-sheet/induced-abortion-united-states

https://www.cdc.gov/mmwr/volumes/67/ss/ss6713a1.htm#T7_down

https://www.webmd.com/baby/guide/third-trimester

https://www.nytimes.com/2005/06/19/books/chapters/the-ethical-brain.html

https://en.wikipedia.org/wiki/Roe_v._Wade#Legal

https://www.reuters.com/article/us-florida-shooting-anniversary-poll/americans-support-gun-control-but-doubt-lawmakers-will-act-reuters-ipsos-poll-idUSKCN1PX11I

https://news.gallup.com/poll/1576/abortion.aspx

https://www.cnn.com/2019/05/15/politics/new-york-gun-control-supreme-court/index.html

https://en.wikipedia.org/wiki/District_of_Columbia_v._Heller

https://www.thedailybeast.com/the-nra-just-reported-losing-dollar55-million-in-income

https://www.brennancenter.org/analysis/his-own-words-presidents-attacks-courts

https://news.gallup.com/poll/1576/abortion.aspx

https://www.usatoday.com/story/news/politics/2019/04/24/donald-trump-says-hell-fight-impeachment-supreme-court/3559509002/

15. "Trump cares about me."

https://www.bustle.com/p/trumps-i-hear-you-note-to-himself-during-the-white-house-listening-session-is-eye-wateringly-awkward-8293884

https://www.thedailybeast.com/trump-gets-gentle-reassurance-from-twitter-chief-jack-dorsey-over-follower-count-in-white-house-meeting

https://theweek.com/speedreads/813387/6-notsocharitable-things-trumps-charity-spent-money

https://news.artnet.com/art-world/trump-painting-1475962

;) A and E

Made in the
USA
Middletown, DE